2

from CHAMBERS

consisting of:

Last Summer at Bluefish Cove

and

A LATE SNOW

two of JANE CHAMBERS' most popular plays
in one convenient volume from

T 'n' T Classics , Inc.

BOOKS

T 'n' T

are explosive!

360 West 36 St. #2NW
NEW YORK N .Y. 10018-6412
212-736-6279; FAX: 212-695-3219

2 from CHAMBERS

FIRST EDITION June 1998
COVER DESIGN by LEON MUNIER
photo credit: **Beth Allen**

**Library of Congress Catalog card number:
97-60649**
ISBN 1-886586-04-7

LAST SUMMER AT BLUEFISH COVE

Library of Congress cataloguing in publication data:
Chambers, Jane 1937-1983
Last Summer at Bluefish Cove.

    (The JH Press gay play script series)
    I. Title II. Series
    PS3553,H258L3   812'.54   81-86655
    ISBN 0-935672-04-4   AACR2
    ISBN 0-935672-05-2 (pbk)

A LATE SNOW

Copyright   1970 by Jane Chambers

First JH Press edition, January 1989

Library of Congress Cataloging-in-publication Data

Chambers, Jane (1937-1983)
    A Late Snow: a play by Jane Chambers
        p.cm. - (The JH Press gay play script series)
    ISBN 0-935672-14-1:
    I. Title   II. Series
ps3553.H258l34   1988   812'.54   88-13294
                        CIP

LAST SUMMER AT BLUEFISH COVE
and A LATE SNOW

A WORD FROM THE PUBLISHER:

These were two plays by Ms. Chambers with which I was
closely affiliated, and so they have a very special meaning
for me,. I was the publicist on the production before it
moved and at Actors Playhouse Off-Broadway of *LAST
SUMMER AT BLUEFISH COVE*, and the director of the
Meridian Gay Theatre Off-Broadway Production of *A LATE
SNOW.*

I also publicized *MY BLUE HEAVEN* when it was presented at the Shandol, and directed a condensed version of
her final play, *KUDZU*, which I hope to publish in the near
future.

Ms.Chambers, whose heart was wider than the range of her
published work, and whose friendship and affection were
felt by many, including myself, was an extraordinary writer
and human being, and it is my hope that her work will live
forever. To that end, I am proud to publish two of her most
beloved plays in this one volume.

Francine L. Trevens, President
T'n'T Classics, Inc.

Last Summer
at Bluefish Cove

A PLAY IN TWO ACTS BY

Jane Chambers

reprinted from the
JH PRESS
GAY PRESS SCRIPT SERIES

by

T 'n' T CLASSICS, INC.

BOOKS

are explosive

360 WEST 36 ST. #2NW
NEW YORK NY 10018-6412
212-736-6279: FAX - 212-695-3219

Jane Chambers

began her career in the '50's as both actress and playwright. Her plays have been produced Off-Broadway, in regional and community theatre here and abroad, and on T. V. She was the recipient of a number of awards including The Connecticut Educational Television Award (1971) a Eugene O'Neill fellowship (1972) a National Writer's Guild Award (1973) and from 1980-83 The Villager Award, the New York Dramalogue Critic's Circle Award, the Alliance for Lesbian and Gay Artists Media Award, the Robby Award, the Oscar Wilde Award, the L.A. Drama Critic's Circle Award and a proclamation from L.A. for outstanding theatre; The Betty Award twice, and in 1982 the Human Dignity Award.

Published novels include BURNING* and CHASIN' JASON*. Her articles appeared in publications such as the New York Times and Harpers. Published plays are *MY BLUE HEAVEN, A LATE SNOW, LAST SUMMER AT BLUEFISH COVE* and *EYE OF THE GULL* (Heinemann Books.) Published poetry includes a volume of her works, WARRIOR AT REST* and selected poems in GAY AND LESBIAN POETRY OF OUR TIME (St. Martin's Press.)

A founding member of the New Jersey Women's Political Caucus and Interart Theatre, NYC, she was on the planning committee of the Women's Project of the American Theatre Association and a member of Writer's Guild East and East End Gay Organization for Human Rights. She taught in women's study, writing and acting programs in universities throughout the U. S.

On February 18, 1983 she died of a brain tumor at her Greenport, L.I. home, survived by her mother, two step-brothers and her life companion, Beth Allen. In 1983 the Jane Chambers Memorial Playwrighting Award was established.

*available from T 'n' T CLASSICS, INC.

Jane Chambers

This play is lovingly and gratefully dedicated to IRENE TRAVIS
without whom there would have been no productiion

PRODUCTION HISTORY

LAST SUMMER AT BLUEFISH COVE was first produced by The Glines, opening February 13, 1980 at the Shandol Theatre, Manhattan, where it ran for twelve performances. Lawrence Lane, Executive Producer; Billy Blackwell, Producer; Directed by Harriet Leider; Sets by Tony Allicino; Lights by Debra Weiser; Stage Manager, Yvonne Fisher; Theme: "Impatient Heart" by Marcia Malamet and Peter Allen. In the cast were: Jean Smart (Lil,) Madelyn Albert (Eva,) Ellie Schadt (Kitty,) Aphroditi Kolaitis (Annie,) Madeline Welsing (Rae,) Janet Morrison (Rita,) Stephanie Rula (Sue,) Karen Sederholm (Donna.)

On June 3, 1980 LAST SUMMER....opened at West Side Mainstage, Manhattan, as part of the First American Gay Arts Festival, produced by The Glines, for a limited run of eight weeks; it was extended an additional four weeks, Lawrence Lane, Executive Producer; Jerry Thomas, Producer; Directed by Nyla Lyon; Sets by Michael C. Smith; Lighting Design by Carol Sealey; Costumes by Joyce Ostrin; Production Stage Manager, Steve Zorthian*; Assistant Stage Manager, Sandra Soehngen. Theme Song, "Impatient Heart:" by Marcia Malamet and Peter Allen. Publicity by FLT. In the cast:

LIL	Jean Smart
EVA	Carolyn Cope
KITTY	Anita Keal**
ANNIE	Aphroditi Kolaitis
RAE	Madeline Welsing
RITA	Janet Morrison
DONNA	Karen Sederholm***
SUE	Stephanie Rula

Understudies: Mercedes Ruehl, Sandra Soehngen (*Replaced by Grant Brown;
**replaced by Dolores Kenan; ***replaced by Elizabeth Wingate.)

On December 2, 1980, LAST SUMMER...began previews at the Actors Playhouse, New York City. Produced by John Glines and Lawrence Lane presenting The Glines production. Opened Dec. 22, 1980; closed Marsh 1, 1981. Director: Nyla Lyon; Sets: Reagan Cook; Lighting Design: Jeffrey Schissler; Costumes: Giva Taylor; Production Stage Manager: Paula Ellen Cohen*, Assistant Stage Manager, Laura Burroughs. In the cast:

LIL	Diane Tarleton**
EVA	Susan Slavin
KITTY	Janet Sarno
ANNIE	Holly Barron***
RAE	Lauren Craig
RITA	Dulcie Arnold
DONNA	Robin Mary Paris
SUE	Celia Howard

Understudies: Holly Barron, Caroline Aaron, Lauren Craig, Margaret Ritchie, Carolyn Cope, Jane Chambers. (*Replaced by Peter Pope; ** replaced by Jean Smart, Holly Barron, Caroline Aaron; ***replaced by Susan Blomhaert.)

ACT ONE

(Early summer at Bluefish Cove, an isolated beach area near the city. In the foreground, there is a pebble beach. At the apron, a jutting rock rears its head above the sea, speckled with seaweed and colonies of clutching mussels. Upstage, a flight of weathered wooden steps lead to a one-room rustic cabin with a living/sleeping area and a kitchenette. A door leads off the room to an unseen bathroom. There is also a door to a closet, upstage.

At rise, the cottage is dimly lit and our attention is focused on the rock and beach. A pair of rubber sandals and a well-worn workshirt are tossed carelessly at the foot of the steps. On the rock, barefoot, clad in worn cutoffs and frayed halter is LIL ZALINSKI, sitting [or standing] and squinting into the afternoon sun as she waits impatiently for a fish to bite. From her handling of the pole, we can see she is an experienced fisherwoman.)

LIL: Come on, you mother, bite. *(Pause.)* I see you circling down there. Come on, sweetheart. *(She jiggles bait.)* Damn. You obviously don't know who you're dealing with here. I won the 1960 All American Girl Scout Fish-Off. I was the champeen. Sixteen bass and twelve blowfish. Of course I was just a kid then but I've gotten better with the years. *(She pulls in the line, checks the bait.)*

(EVA MARGOLIS enters, unseen by LIL. EVA is walking quietly along the beach. She is dressed in proper resort clothing— everything about her says upper middle class. She watches LIL, unseen, with interest and amusement.)

LIL: *(Wiggles line.)* If you were a person, you know what we'd call you? A C.T. You nuzzle the bait but you don't put out. Now, I'm going to try a different approach, it's called courting. You're going to love it. Here's how it goes. You're a terrific looking fish, you know that, sweetheart? You're a real knockout. Now, don't get me wrong, it's not just your body I'm after. I love your mind, your sense of humor, your intellect, your politics. . . . Aha, I'm getting your attention, huh? I respect you, darling. I love you. Now, bite, baby, bite.

(EVA who, unnoticed by LIL, has been listening, speaks.)

EVA: I'd fall for that. It's a good line.

LIL: *(Surprised.)* Would you mind telling that to the bluefish? *(She notes that EVA is an attractive woman and turns on the charm.)* I usually do pretty well with that line, I must be losing my touch.

EVA: *(Not picking up on LIL's flirtatiousness.)* Maybe you need to change your strategy. *(She walks to water's edge and peers in at fish.)* You could try caveman tactics. Hit it on the head with a stick.

LIL: *(Still charming.)* Not my style. I prefer a classier approach.

EVA: *(Still innocent.)* Have you tried poetry? *(To fish.)* "Shall I compare thee to a summer's day? Thou art more lovely and more temperate."

LIL: *(Peers into water.)* It's gone. Gone. You've driven that fish right back to the Atlantic.

EVA: *(Shrugs.)* As my mother always tells me, there are other fish in the sea.

LIL: That's a practical philosophy. Coldhearted but practical.

EVA: You're getting a bad sunburn. Is that your shirt? Better put it on.

(EVA *picks up* LIL's *shirt from the steps, tosses it to her.* LIL *takes this as a sign of interest from* EVA *but* EVA *is only being friendly and proceeds to exit down the beach.)*

LIL: Thanks.

EVA: *(Going.)* Don't lose heart. Maybe you'll catch that fish tomorrow.

LIL: Hey— *(EVA turns.)* I'm Lillian Zalinski. Everybody calls me Lil.

EVA: Eva Margolis. I'm the pink cabin for the summer. *(She continues to leave.)*

LIL: *(Trying to stop her.)* Holly House. We call it Holly House. I'm in Crabapple, right up there. We've all been wondering who rented Holly House this season. The couple who had it the last two years split up. You're the only newcomer on the Cove this year, the other cabins are the same old gang. Are you alone?

EVA: Yes. The other cabins are all rented to couples?

LIL: *(Meaning herself.)* All but one.

EVA: I guess I'll have to get used to being odd man out.

LIL: More like New Girl In Town. You'll get lots of attention, I guarantee it.

EVA: *(Still misunderstanding.)* Well, I could use some attention. You're married, of course?

LIL: Not me. I'm the other one who's not a couple.

(EVA senses that LIL is not an ordinary person—that there is some subtext in this repartee but she can't identify it, so she asks:)

EVA: Are you one of those swinging singles I've read about?

LIL: *(Teasing.)* Well, that depends . . .

EVA: *(Thinking she's got it.)* I bet you're an artist—or a writer!

LIL: No. I used to sell time for a television station—but I'm taking the summer off.

EVA: You and I are the only singles?

LIL: That's right. *(LIL, of course, is pleased at that.)*

EVA: *(Disappointed.)* Well, it's going to be a long summer. I hope you play chess. *(She starts to leave again.)*

LIL: I hate it. I like to fish.

EVA: You can't fish at night.

LIL: I could fish at night but I prefer to do more interesting things. *(EVA still looks blank.)* Hey, would you toss me those sandals? This beach is murder on the feet. *(EVA brings her the sandals.)* You'll have to come to the opening of the season bash tonight. It's at my cabin, right up there. Music, food, booze, dancing. *(EVA is trying to size LIL up.)*

EVA: Were you ever married?

LIL: *(Cavalierly.)* Oh, sure. Lots of times.

EVA: I was only married once. For twelve years.

LIL: *(Stunned.)* Twelve years? I had one that made it two years and eight months. Eight long months. Rae and Annie will approve of you. They've been together nine.

EVA: How many times were you really married?

LIL: Oh God, I don't know—a dozen? Who counts?

EVA: Come on. A dozen husbands?

LIL: *(Realizing.)* Husbands?

EVA: Husbands. You know the guy in the tuxedo, he's waiting at the altar when you come down the aisle.

LIL: Husbands.

EVA: Husbands.

LIL: How did you come to rent Holly House?

EVA: Oh, it was a godsend. I walked out on George on Wednesday, just packed the suitcases and left. It gave me such pleasure to leave him stranded with a paisley overnight bag and a Board of Directors meeting in Chicago the next day. He'd go naked before he'd carry a paisley bag into a Board of Directors meeting —no, he wouldn't go naked. He thinks he's underdeveloped—for all I know, he may be. I married him when I was still in college so my basis for comparison is limited. Is six inches small? This book I'm reading says size doesn't matter. It's all in how he uses it. Foreplay is everything—this book says. It's called *The Female Sexual Imperative.* It's written by a woman doctor. Have you read it?

LIL: *(Still stunned.)* I've seen it.

EVA: *(Enjoying this conversation.)* Well, you probably know everything that's in it, anyway. I can't believe I've gotten to be this old and I don't know anything.

LIL: How did you get Holly House?

EVA: I left George on Wednesday and drove until dark. I wasn't heading any place in particular, I was just leaving George. I wound up in the village over there and checked into the Holiday Inn. The desk clerk—he was one of those sweet young men, you know the kind—handed me the room key and I burst into tears. I realized that I was going to spend the night alone, away from home, for the first time in my life.

LIL: How did you get *here*?

EVA: To Bluefish Cove? Well, the desk clerk—actually, he was quite nice in spite of his predilections—he said there was a place right down the street where I could get a drink and not be approached by mashers, a place where mostly businesswomen went. . . .

LIL: He sent you to Molly Pitcher's?

EVA: And I met this nice lady at the bar—she's a real estate agent—

LIL: Margery Eaton.

EVA: She handles the rentals for Bluefish Cove. I suppose you know her.

LIL: Very well.

EVA: I told her I needed quiet, some place to get myself to-gether—she was wonderful. She didn't question me or ask for references, she didn't even ask me if I had a husband or kids. She just took my money and handed me the lease. I think she's a feminist. She assumed I was in charge of my own life.

LIL: She assumed something, that's for sure.

EVA: And it's working out wonderfully. It's beautiful here—and maybe I'll make some new friends. This party tonight, it's at your cabin?

LIL: *(Quickly.)* But you don't have to come.

EVA: Oh, but I want to. I've been holed up in my cabin for days now reading *The Female Sexual Imperative*. A party tonight would be just perfect, Lil. It's time for me to make my debut as a single woman.

LIL: *(Trying to ease out gracefully.)* Eva, you might feel out of place.

EVA: *(Misunderstanding.)* Because I'm single? Well, you are, too. Of course, I've been married so long I've forgotten how to flirt—but then you said it's mostly couples here—still, some-body might have a single houseguest or a bachelor brother, you never know, we might get lucky. I don't even remember how to hold a conversation with a man. *(She sees that* LIL *is un-comfortable.)* I promise not to cut in on your territory.

LIL: Somehow I'm not worried about that. It's just a bunch of beach bums, just the residents of the Cove. It's no big thing.

EVA: It is to me. I'm going to a party—by myself! I feel like a teenager again. When I was in high school, my best friend Joan and I always had a pow-wow before going to a party— I would never have dreamed of picking out a dress—or a boy-friend—without getting Joan's approval first. *(Touching* LIL*'s hand.)* This book is right. It is possible for grown women to be friends. *(She feels slightly awkward at the sudden closeness and turns to leave.)* Thank you, Lil. I'll see you tonight!

LIL: *(As* EVA *goes,* LIL *glances toward the cabin.)* Oh, dear. Oh, dear.

(Lights go down on the beach. LIL *sits on the steps in the darkness and begins to clean fish quietly. We do not notice her because the lights go up in the cabin—there is music and chatter.* ANNIE *and* RAE *are dancing,* KITTY *paces as* RITA *watches. It is several hours later.)*

KITTY: Damn Marge Eaton!

RITA: She might have been drunk.

RAE: I think she made a perfectly reasonable assumption.

ANNIE: Walks like a duck, talks like a duck, hangs out with ducks, must be a duck.

KITTY: How could Marge do this to me?

RAE: If you meet a woman in a gay bar, you naturally assume she's gay.

KITTY: This could ruin my career!

RAE: Annie has just as much to lose as you have, Kitty. Annie's famous, too.

ANNIE: Rae . . .

RAE: Well, you are, darling. Annie was famous when you *(Meaning* KITTY.) were still delivering babies at that clinic in Brooklyn.

KITTY: It's not the same thing. Annie's a sculptor.

RAE: Sculptress. We take pride in the feminine gender.

KITTY: Well, you shouldn't. It's diminutive. Sculptor is generic. And nobody cares who a sculptor . . .

RAE: Sculptress.

ANNIE: Honey . . .

KITTY: Who a sculptor goes to bed with.

RITA: Kitty is developing a new language. She's going to write a dictionary of nonsexist language.

KITTY: *(To* ANNIE.) Nobody cares who you go to bed with.

RAE: I do. (RAE *turns off the record player, busies herself in the kitchen.* ANNIE *tends the bar.)*

KITTY: I have a new book coming out!

RITA: It's even better than *The Female Sexual Imperative.* It's called *Coming Together: The Search for Connubial Equality.* It's a play on words.

KITTY: I'm trying to liberate American women.

RITA: *Publisher's Weekly* gave her an award. "Literature's Most Credible Women's Libber."

ANNIE: Don't worry, Kitty. If your career blows up, we'll give you an award. *(She hands* KITTY *a drink.)* "Bluefish Cove's Most Incredible Dyke."

KITTY: It isn't funny. I'll lose my credibility.

ANNIE: Not to mention your royalties.

KITTY: I'm dependent on my royalties! *(About* RITA.*)* We're dependent on my royalties. I gave up a career in medicine, remember, to devote myself to The Movement.

RAE: Why is it every time Kitty says "The Movement," it sounds like a disturbance of the lower colon?

KITTY: I don't know why I come back here every summer— I don't know why I put up with the bunch of you—I'm dedicating my life to a worthy cause—

RITA: We didn't have to come here this summer. The Swedish government offered Kitty a grant to go there and write.

ANNIE: Kitty, m'dear, we are your old friends. We recognize

that you gave up long gory hours in the operating room in order to make a million writing books; we recall how you sacrificed day after day of peering up dark vaginas with a penlight in order to become a national celebrity. Our hearts bleed for you when we see your handsome face on the cover of *Ms.* or tune into Phil Donahue and listen to you instructing American women to grab their sexuality—

RAE: No, honey. "Seize their sexuality," that's what she said on Donahue. "Seize your sexuality," she said. Some woman in the audience thought she was advocating masturbation.

RITA: She does advocate masturbation. There's a whole chapter on it in this new book.

ANNIE: We are aware of your achievements and cognizant of your sacrifices. We have watched you fall in and out of love, in and out of lust, in and out of hangovers, we have tolerated and accepted you when you were young, dedicated and struggling, we tolerate and accept you now that you are rich, famous and arrogant. Bluefish Cove is more than just a lesbian beach colony, Kitty, it's family. And that's why you keep coming back.

RITA: Kitty is not arrogant. She's brilliant.

ANNIE: She's both. And she depends on us to keep her from becoming totally obnoxious.

KITTY: I wouldn't take that from anybody else, you know.

ANNIE: I know. That's why I said it.

RAE: What are families for?

KITTY: *(Calling out to steps.)* Lil, how can you do this to me? My career is in jeopardy! A straight woman in Bluefish Cove. I can't believe it. Is nothing sacred any more?

ANNIE: Kitty, don't get in a snit and screw up this summer, huh? Have some consideration, will you? *(She nods toward the door where* LIL *sits outside.)*

RAE: It's just one woman. One simple, little woman. She's not going to rent the Goodyear blimp and fly cross-country with a banner announcing that Dr. Kitty Cochrane is a lesbian.

KITTY: It only takes one person to start a rumor that can ruin a career.

ANNIE: Lil has the right to invite anybody she wants, anybody at all, to her own cabin for her own party.

KITTY: What difference does it make to Lil? She hasn't got anything to lose.

RAE: Kitty.

KITTY: I didn't mean it like that. I just mean—we're dealing with the rest of my life.

ANNIE: We're dealing with the rest of Lil's life, too.

RAE: We all agreed we were going to make this summer perfect. Nobody is going to fight—

ANNIE: *(To* KITTY.*)* —or fuck around.

RITA: Kitty never fucks around.

RAE: Love is blind.

ANNIE: *(To* KITTY *and* RITA.*)* Please, think about Lil.

RITA: *(Helpfully.)* Well, maybe it won't be so bad, Kitty. She is a straight woman. She'll be source material for your new book.

KITTY: Well, I can't see any other way of doing this: we'll all just have to pretend we're straight.

(RAE *shakes her head helplessly.* ANNIE, *who has poured a drink for* LIL, *takes both glasses and heads for door, disgusted.)*

ANNIE: I'm just about to give up on you, Kitty.

KITTY: I can say Rita's my cousin.

RITA: You could say I'm your secretary. I am your secretary.

KITTY: But, darling, she's bound to come into our cabin sometime during the summer and celebrities don't sleep in a double bed with their secretaries—but if you're my cousin—

RAE: Incest is preferable to being gay.

KITTY: *(To* RAE.*)* Annie could be your—sister-in-law. You can say you're divorced, which is true, you wouldn't have to lie, and you can say Annie's husband died valiantly in Viet Nam.

Donna can say she's Sue's daughter.

RAE: I don't want to be around when you suggest that to Sue. Sue's slightly paranoid about that age difference, anyway.

RITA: But Kitty, we'd have to lie all the time. I mean, if the woman is living in Holly House, she's going to see us everywhere, every day, on the beach, at the picnic tables, in the glen, on the path . . .

RAE: Kitty, the woman may be straight but I haven't heard that she's retarded.

RITA: I don't know if we could carry it off, Kitty. Someone's bound to make a slip.

KITTY: Oh, shut up, Rita. I know that. They wouldn't do it, anyway. Nobody cares about my career! The whole thing is hideous and impossible. *(She wails and sinks into further depression.)* Sooner or later, it's your friends who do you in. My father used to say that.

(Lights dim on the cabin, up on beach. ANNIE has descended the steps and sits just above LIL.)

ANNIE: Need some help?

LIL: No thanks, I'm almost finished.

ANNIE: Why didn't you have them cleaned at the market?

LIL: How'd you know I didn't catch these?

ANNIE: I was looking out the window this afternoon when you came up the stairs with an empty bucket.

LIL: Don't rat on me. I have a reputation to uphold.

ANNIE: My lips are sealed.

LIL: Actually, I don't mind cleaning them. It releases my hostilities. *(ANNIE hands LIL the drink.)* Thanks. Has Kitty offended anyone yet?

ANNIE: Everyone. Right off.

LIL: Good. It's the opening of the season initiation. Kitty offends everyone, everyone puts Kitty in her place. Then we can settle in for the long, hot summer. Same thing, every year. When I lived with Kitty, it was a nightly ritual, putting Kitty in her place. She thrives on it, you know.

ANNIE: She's having a temper tantrum about your asking the straight lady to the party tonight.

LIL: I never would have if I'd known she was straight—but by the time I found out, it was too late. Well, she'll have to face it sooner or later—she might as well know right now, at the beginning of the season, she's smack in the middle of a bunch of dykes.

ANNIE: Kitty would prefer she never finds that out.

LIL: Kitty may change her mind when she sees her. She's nice looking.

ANNIE: I saw her. From the window.

LIL: Ah-ah.

ANNIE: Not me. I'm a married lady.

LIL: Maybe she'll turn out to be a nice, straight lady for Kitty to chase around after all summer. Kitty has never made it through a summer at Bluefish Cove without at least one side affair.

ANNIE: Not true. She never fooled around the two years she lived with you. You were the one who fooled around.

LIL: She called me an alley cat.

ANNIE: I remember. You had that fling with Donna. . . .

LIL: But I denied it. I swore, Girl-Scout's Honor, I hadn't laid a finger on Donna.

ANNIE: She didn't believe you. Kitty may be a pain in the ass but she's nobody's fool.

LIL: She set the answering machine to monitor and record. She bugged our goddam telephone.

ANNIE: And you, dummy, made a date to meet Donna at a motel—

LIL: Well, where else? She was living with Sue, I was living with Kitty—I'm too old to do it in the back of a car.

ANNIE: Didn't Kitty follow you to the motel?

LIL: Pounded on the door, made a complete ass of herself. Donna and I jumped out the window, bare-assed, with our clothes under our arms. Good thing we were on the first floor.

ANNIE: And Kitty never let you back in your apartment.

LIL: Never. Changed the locks and put my things out in the hallway like an Indian matriarch divorcing her husband.

ANNIE: You ever wish you'd stayed with Kitty?

LIL: It never would have worked.

ANNIE: It might have. I wouldn't have believed, nine years ago, that Rae and I would make it—but we have. And it's better now than it ever was.

LIL: *(Shrugs.)* I'm not a long-distance runner, Annie.

ANNIE: You were in love with Kitty.

LIL: Oh, for a minute, maybe. But I had a lust for freedom and she had a lust for fame and fortune. . . . Kitty's all right. Don't go so hard on her.

ANNIE: I'll try to remember that.

LIL: Someday sculptures by Anne Joseph will be in the Metropolitan and dedicated little art students will pry into your life, long-nosed intense professors will refer to you as the Master of Free Form. . . .

ANNIE: You think so?

LIL: I know it. And books by Dr. Kitty Cochrane will be on library shelves a hundred years from now. How long will your sculptures last?

ANNIE: *(Uneasily.)* Indefinitely.

LIL: Thousands of years. And Rae has two grown children and they'll have children. That's a kind of immortality. *(Pause.)* Alley cats just come and go.

(LIL *stands with the bucket and fish heads and bones, then runs down the steps onto the beach, tossing the fish remains against the rock, into the sea.* ANNIE *watches her with love and sadness.)*

ANNIE: Hey, Lil! *(LIL looks up.)* I love you.

LIL: *(Laughs and starts to climb the stairs.)* Don't you start that. We made a pact years ago in a dormitory room, never lovers, always friends.

ANNIE: I didn't mean that, dummy. I only meant you're my good buddy and I love you.

LIL: Come on, cut the crap. How many drinks have you had?

(Lights rise on cabin. RAE *opens the door for them.)*

RAE: I hope you didn't bring the heads and guts in with you.

LIL: Nope. Threw them in the sea. From the sea we come, to the sea we returneth. . . .

RAE: I don't mind cooking them but I sure hate to clean them. *(RAE takes fish, goes about preparing them.)*

LIL: *(Patting RAE's ass.)* Just like a woman.

ANNIE: Watch that, buddy.

RAE: There's nothing more disgusting than a male chauvinist dyke.

   (LIL and ANNIE go into living room.)

LIL: *(Approaching* KITTY *from behind.)* Don't tell me! Yes! It must be! It is! Dr. Kitty Cochrane, High Priestess of Feminism, right in my very own living room. May I have your autograph? *(*KITTY *looks at her coolly.)* Come on, Kitty.

RITA: She's upset that you invited that straight woman.

LIL: Eva? She's just a nice, naive little lady, Kitty. We're going to be a lot more upsetting to her than she is to us.

ANNIE: Ah, but she has invaded our secret Isle of Lesbos. The enemy is in our camp, a traitor moves among us. . . .

RITA: Kitty does have to be very careful.

LIL: She seems like a nice woman. She's all right, Kitty, it's going to be okay. *(Pause.)* Knock, knock, Kitty, can you hear me through the closet door?

KITTY: If this woman blows my cover, if she goes to the media and announces Dr. Kitty Cochrane is a dyke *(She wags her finger at* LIL*)* do you know how David Susskind would love to get hold of that?

LIL: Deny it, Kitty. Deny everything. You're so good at that.

KITTY: The public is not ready. The public is still trying to accept the concepts of equal rights and the clitoral orgasm. It would be a catastrophe for me to come out of the closet now. It would be as incredible as if—Gloria Steinem announced her intention to marry—Marlo Thomas. The entire Movement would shudder and collapse.

RITA: Kitty is a figurehead, jutting boldly and courageously from the prow of the ship of human rights sailing through the treacherous sea of prejudice and ignorance. . . .

LIL: *(To* KITTY.*)* You didn't write that?

RITA: Yes, she did.

KITTY: I didn't use it. It was a first draft. Rita, how could you remember that?

RITA: I remember everything you write, Kitty. I have to type it four times. She does four drafts of everything. .

LIL: *(To* KITTY.*)* I think I liked you better when you practiced medicine. You always looked so sexy in that white coat. *(LIL, tired, sits.)*

KITTY: How're you feeling, Lil?

LIL: Terrific.

KITTY: Really.

LIL: Don't start on me. You're not my doctor.

KITTY: You're under my supervision.

LIL: Bullshit. You have my records, that's all. I only agreed to that because my doctor wouldn't let me spend the summer out here otherwise. If I suddenly turn fuschia and collapse, do something. Otherwise, keep your distance, understand?

RITA: Kitty just wants to help you.

LIL: *(To* KITTY.*)* You don't even practice medicine any more.

RITA: She didn't go to Sweden this summer so she could stay here with you.

KITTY: Rita! That's not true, Lil. I never did like Sweden and I wouldn't miss a summer at the Cove for anything. *(She feels* LIL's *forehead.)* You're overdoing. You cannot stay on that beach all day. You can't take that much sun.

LIL: You try to take my pulse and I'll break your fingers. I'm fine. I feel just fine.

(EVA *is approaching on the beach.*)

RAE: Hey, here she comes.

ANNIE: *(Wiggling her eyebrows.)* Nice. Very nice. You always did have good taste, Lil.

RAE: *(To* ANNIE.*)* Get in here and butter this skillet before I break it over your head.

ANNIE: I love a possessive woman.

RAE: Well, you've got one. *(About* EVA.*)* She's skinny and she's got blue eyes—and if I catch you looking crocksided at her, I'll snatch you baldheaded.

EVA: *(Calling.)* Lil?

ANNIE: *(At the door.)* You've got the right place. Come on up.

RAE: *(To* ANNIE.*)* You're a married woman.

ANNIE: I can dream, can't I?

RAE: Skinny with blue eyes. Revs up her motor every time. Get in here. *(She hauls* ANNIE *in by her britches pocket. This is a game between* RAE *and* ANNIE. *They are devoted to each other.)*

EVA: *(At door.)* Lil?

(LIL, who shows evidence of being tired, goes to the door.)

LIL: Hi, Eva.

EVA: I didn't hear much noise but I was too excited to wait. I've been dressed and ready for an hour.

LIL: Donna and Sue are late, as usual, but everybody else is here. Come on in.

EVA: Do I look all right?

ANNIE: I think you look terrific. *(To RAE.)* Doesn't she look terrific?

RAE: Wonderful.

KITTY: *(Inside, to RITA.)* I hope she doesn't introduce us by last names.

RAE: *(Wipes her hand on towel and extends it.)* I'm Rae. Welcome to Bluefish Cove. The Li'l Abner character here is Annie Joseph.

ANNIE: Hi. We've been looking forward to meeting you. Lil told us all about you.

LIL: Not all. I don't know everything.

ANNIE: Hey, what are you drinking? Besides being assistant

chef, I'm also the official barkeep.

EVA: Scotch and water, do you have that?

ANNIE: Sure. Coming up.

LIL: Rita Sanderson, Eva Margolis.

EVA: Hi.

KITTY: *(Quickly.)* I'm Katherine.

EVA: Hello.

ANNIE: You want this Scotch heavy or light?

EVA: Oh, light, please, I'm not a big drinker. Did you say your name is Annie Joseph?

ANNIE: That's right.

EVA: Are you the sculptress?

KITTY: Sculp*tor*.

ANNIE: It doesn't matter. I make sculptures.

EVA: I took a class in art appreciation last year—we studied you.

ANNIE: Thank you.

EVA: I never met a sculptress *(She hesitates, anxious to please, and glances towards* KITTY*'s back.)*—sculptor?— *(But* KITTY *doesn't respond.)* —before.

RITA: *(Being helpful.)* Sculptress sounds like she does a little less of it a little less well.

RAE: Bull!

KITTY: *(To* RAE.*)* We really need a new word altogether. We need to develop our own language.

EVA: *(To* KITTY.*)* You must be a feminist! I'm trying to become one. I'm reading that new book by Dr. Cochrane right now: *The Female Sexual Imperative.* *(*KITTY *has turned her face away from* EVA, *so* EVA *addresses* ANNIE.*)* Have you read it?

ANNIE: *(To* LIL.*)* Do I have to answer that?

EVA: Oh, do. You'll love it. It'll change your life. I know most men get very uptight about their wives reading feminist literature —George nearly went wild when I bought this book by Dr. Cochrane. He said his secretary read it and got so uppity he had to fire her. And of course he blames Dr. Cochrane and her book for the fact I left him.

RAE: It wouldn't be the first time Dr. Cochrane's been blamed for a breakup.

EVA: But it's not true. It's really not. I would have eventually left, anyway. I mean, our marriage just wasn't working. We tried everything. We really did. *(To* RITA.*)* Have you read Dr. Cochrane's book?

RITA: Well, yes, I have.

EVA: She's wonderful.

RITA: She's marvelous.

EVA: I would have left George anyway but Dr. Cochrane's book made me feel good about it—as if it were a beginning, not an end.

KITTY: What a lovely thing to say.

RITA: *(To* ANNIE.*)* You see? She is a figurehead, jutting boldly and courageously from the prow of the ship of human rights.

EVA: She's the most important woman in the twentieth century, that's what I think. Kitty Cochrane is going to change the world.

ANNIE: *(To* LIL.*)* She can't hold out against this kind of flattery —I give her fifteen more minutes.

LIL: Fifteen more seconds. Bet you ten bucks.

EVA: If any of you haven't read the book, I'll let you have my copy when I'm finished. Just don't tell your husbands where you got it from. I'm in the last chapter now and I have savored every word. I'm telling you, you don't know what it is to be a woman until you've read Dr. Kitty Cochrane.

KITTY: I'm really thrilled the book has had such meaning for you.

LIL: *(Nudges* ANNIE.*)* See?

EVA: Oh, it has. It saved my life.

KITTY: Really?

EVA: Oh, *yes*.

LIL: *(To* ANNIE.*)* Watch this. *(*KITTY *hesitates a moment.)* Now.

KITTY: I am Dr. Kitty Cochrane.

LIL: *(To* ANNIE.*)* Ten bucks. Fork over.

EVA: *(Stunned.)* Really?

RITA: But Kitty, you said . . .

KITTY: Rita, I have an obligation to my public.

EVA: How terribly exciting.

(RAE, *who has missed much of the previous interchange because she was taking food out of the oven, rises, plates in hand.)*

RAE: *(Handing out plates.)* Okay, group, soup's on.

EVA: But everybody's not here. . . .

RAE: Like I used to say to my kids, you get here on time or your plate goes in the oven.

EVA: *(To* RAE.*)* When is your husband coming?

RAE: My husband? Coming? Oh, he's not. He won't be here. We were divorced nine years ago.

EVA: Oh. What about your children?

RAE: What about them?

ANNIE: They're on their own. One of them's bumming around Oregon and the other one's in summer school in the city.

EVA: You have children, too?

ANNIE: No, I just feel like Rae's are half mine.

EVA: *(Befuddled.)* You're neighbors.

RAE: No, we live together.

EVA: Oh. I don't have children now. We had a son but— *(To* KITTY, *who is cringing.)* —you have children?

KITTY: Oh, no, I don't. *(Quickly.)* I delivered 273 of them, however, and what a glorious thing it is to bring new life into the world.

RITA: I almost had a baby once. *(Everyone stares at her, surprised.)* I was pregnant when I was in college. The boy was very considerate. He paid for the abortion. It was a little girl.

EVA: I used to want a little girl. I wanted her to look just like me. My immortality, I guess. *(To* KITTY.*)* Your book says a woman has the right to control her own body. My husband, George, thinks that's a mortal sin. George thinks a lot of things are mortal sins. Like the things you say in your book about marital sex—

(The lights are fading on that scene and coming up on the beach where SUE, *a homely woman in her mid-40s, is helping* DONNA, *a beauty in her 20s, cross the rocky beach.* SUE *is obviously old money and wears frayed jeans and torn sneakers with the ease of the very rich.* DONNA *is very conscious of her good looks. She's a flirt and a social climber and does both with charm.)*

DONNA: Wait, Sue!

SUE: Honey, I told you that you couldn't walk this beach in those sandals. If you'd wear sensible sneakers. . . .

DONNA: The sandals make my ankles look thinner.

SUE: If your ankles got any thinner, your feet would break off. Come on.

DONNA: The sandals are sexier. Too bad Gucci isn't imprinted on the back of them.

SUE: I could stamp Saks Fifth Avenue on your ass.

DONNA: I'd like to have a pair of these in white, too. Can we order them by phone?

SUE: On one condition. Don't flirt with Lil tonight.

DONNA: Flirt with Lil?

SUE: Don't look dumb. You always flirt with Lil.

DONNA: Oh, Sue.

SUE: Ever since you had that brief affair with her . . .

DONNA: I never had an affair with Lil.

SUE: Don't lie to me. Kitty told me all about it. You and Lil leaping out a motel window.

DONNA: Kitty made up that story.

SUE: Why would Kitty make up a story like that?

DONNA: I don't know but she did. Why on earth would I want Lil Zalinski when I've got you? I bet Lil never made more than fifteen thousand dollars a year in her whole life.

SUE: She's good looking. She's reputed to be dynamite in the sack. She had you once and dropped you like a hot potato. My baby doesn't like to get dumped.

DONNA: They have these sandals in blue, too.

SUE: Have a heart, will you?

DONNA: I saw a terrific denim pantsuit in Lord & Taylor.

SUE: Whatever you want, Donna, just don't flirt with Lil tonight. I may be a fool but I don't want to look like one. Leave me some pride, huh?

DONNA: Don't you even feel sorry for Lil? Don't you feel guilty? You're ten years older than she is and you're still healthy as a horse.

SUE: When you're born into my financial bracket, you feel sorry for everybody, guilty about everything—and you learn very quickly that you can't do a damn thing about other people's bad luck. Two pairs of sandals and a pantsuit, that's all you want? You have a tragic flaw, Donna. You never gamble for high enough stakes. I might have gone for a Mercedes. *(She pats* DONNA's *rump.)* Keep moving, honey. We're late already. Go on.

DONNA: *(Climbing steps.)* YOO-HOO!

SUE: *(As they enter.)* Only an hour late, we're improving.

RAE: Come on in, your plates are in the oven.

ANNIE: *(To* EVA.*)* They're always late. Donna has to change clothes twenty times.

EVA: I changed clothes four times tonight, myself.

RAE: Sue McMillan, Donna Atterly, Eva Margolis. Eva's got Holly House this season.

SUE: Welcome. The two who had it last year fought nightly,

kept the whole Cove in a state of crisis. I hope you're happily paired up with someone.

EVA: No, I'm not. *(DONNA takes an interested look.)*

SUE: Oh, dear. I was hoping for some peace and quiet.

RITA: Eva just broke up—

SUE: Well, we've all been through that—

RITA: With her husband. She's been married for twelve years.

DONNA: To a man?

EVA: What else? *(There is an awkward silence.)* Well, don't worry, I won't burden you with the boring details. Other people's divorces are a dull subject of conversation.

RAE: We were just discussing our children.

DONNA: Children?

RAE: Well, I do have two, you know.

EVA: *(To DONNA.)* Do you have children?

DONNA: Me?

EVA: Well, I'm sure you will. You're young yet. Are you married?

DONNA: Married? Me?

ANNIE: *(To DONNA.)* You're not married.

DONNA: No, I'm not married.

EVA: But your last name is different from your mother's.

DONNA: My mother?

LIL: She's not her mother.

DONNA: Sue? No, she's not my mother.

EVA: I'm sorry.

SUE: It's all right. It's an understandable mistake.

DONNA: You didn't think it was understandable when the maitre d' at Lutece said it. You nearly bit his head off.

EVA: I'm sorry. I just assumed . . .

SUE: Forget it. All right? *(She moves to the window, embarrassed.)*

ANNIE: Honey, did you put coffee on?

DONNA: *(To EVA.)* Now see what you've done? She'll give me a hard time for the rest of the night.

EVA: I've apologized. I don't know what else to do.

DONNA: Well, it was a dumb thing to say.

LIL: Donna!

EVA: I thought it was a perfectly reasonable assumption. What is she, your aunt?

DONNA: Are you putting me on? *(To* LIL.*)* Where'd you find her?

KITTY: *(Quickly.)* I have a new book coming out. In the fall.

DONNA: *(To* EVA.*)* She's going to give me hell all night because of you.

RITA: Kitty's new book is really very exciting. I've read it, you know. I typed it.

DONNA: Jesus H. Christ. *(She glances toward* SUE.*)*

RAE: *(Seizing the situation.)* Look how clear it is tonight. You can see Connecticut! *(She goes to window and puts her arm around* SUE, *comfortingly.)* I bet it's beautiful from the beach. Lil, why don't you take Eva down and show her the Connecticut skyline from the beach? Coffee will be another ten minutes.

LIL: *(To* EVA.*)* Would you like that?

EVA: *(Anxious to get out of there.)* Yes. Yes, I would.

DONNA: *(To* EVA.*)* You better get your act together or this summer is going to be a real mess.

ANNIE: Be careful on the steps, it's dark and those planks are older than both of you. *(LIL leads EVA down the steps.)*

KITTY: *(Watching them go.)* Dear God in Heaven.

ANNIE: Speak to her for us, Kitty. She listens to you.

KITTY: Sue, you've got to do something about her. *(She means DONNA.)*

DONNA: About me? You better do something about her. Is Lil making it with her or what?

ANNIE: Poor Eva. She doesn't know what the hell is going on.

RAE: It must be awful for her.

DONNA: Awful for her? She hurt Sue's feelings.

SUE: Since when have you cared about that?

DONNA: I care. I've stuck around three years, I must care.

SUE: *(Touched.)* Come on then, give your old Mom a hug and kiss.

DONNA: Just a minute. I want to see what Lil's up to down there.

SUE: That's none of your business.

ANNIE: *(Looking out the window.)* That's what I'd say if they were doing something but they're not doing anything.

KITTY: Give Lil time.

RAE: I don't think that's what Lil has on her mind this summer.

ANNIE: Why not? If I were Lil, that's exactly what I'd have on my mind.

RAE: Kitty? Is she going to make it through the summer?

KITTY: The chemotherapy appears to have had a positive effect. There's no sign of new growth.

ANNIE: So she could get well and live for years.

KITTY: She could.

RITA: But, Kitty, you said that practically never happens, not with that kind of cancer. You said it moves so fast.

KITTY: *(Snaps.)* There is no indication of new growth at the present time.

RITA: But you said . . .

KITTY: It doesn't matter what I said, Rita. The practice of medicine is not an exact science. And I'm no expert in this field, don't ask me!

RITA: You are an expert, Kitty. You were an expert.

KITTY: Never.

RITA: It was your field of specialty!

KITTY: Don't tell me what I did, Rita!

RITA: You said you couldn't stand to watch people dying. You said you had to lie all the time and give people hope when you didn't think there was any.

KITTY: Rita, for God's sake!

RITA: These are your friends, Kitty, and they ought to know— she's not pushy and self-centered the way you think. She's kind and sensitive and caring. . . .

KITTY: Rita, Rita! What am I going to do with you?

RITA: I'm telling them because I love you.

KITTY: I know that! I just don't know how to shut you up!

RITA: She's angry at me that I told her secret.

RAE: It's not a secret, honey.

SUE: It's a charade. She wants us to play it with her, so we do.

DONNA: It's not all a charade. Kitty can be very pushy and self-centered. And mean. She can be very mean.

KITTY: And loud. I can be very loud. You can hear me clear through a motel room door.

DONNA: I haven't the foggiest notion what you're talking about.

RAE: Hold it! RING! Into your corners, ladies. We all agreed no fights this summer. We're going to make this summer perfect: this one's for Lil.

DONNA: What is she doing down there?

SUE: Will you get away from that window?

DONNA: I'm not flirting with her. I'm watching her.

SUE: Well, don't.

RAE: Hey, hey, take it easy, Sue.

DONNA: She can't help herself, she's menopausal.

KITTY: *(Clinically.)* Are you really?

DONNA: She has no interest in sex, she flies off the handle all the time.

RAE: According to Kitty's book, none of those symptoms come with menopause. That's an old wives' tale.

DONNA: Sue says she's menopausal, says it herself.

RAE: Kitty's book says . . .

SUE: Fuck what Kitty's book says. How would Kitty know?

(To KITTY.) Have you *been* menopausal?

KITTY: Don't get so upset, Sue. There's nothing to get so upset about.

SUE: She makes me feel so completely inadequate.

DONNA: I don't make you feel any way—don't blame me for your own insecurities.

ANNIE: *(To* SUE.) Why do you continue to put up with that?

SUE: Because I love her.

DONNA: Do you really? Say that again. I like to hear you say that.

SUE: I can't. Donna, you're driving me crazy! *(SUE exits to bathroom.)*

DONNA: Hey, *wait*! Sue! I was only kidding! Where's your sense of humor?

KITTY: *(At window, looking down at beach.)* I don't like the looks of that.

ANNIE: *(Looking, too.)* Naw, they're just talking.

KITTY: They've been talking too long. Straight ladies can be very dangerous. They tend to toy with our affections.

ANNIE: Well, you're certainly the expert on that subject.

KITTY: *(Starchily.)* Lil does not need to be toyed with this summer.

RITA: I had a college roommate like that. We'd make out all night and then she'd get up in the morning and babble on about how she loved her boyfriend. I thought for months I was hallucinating.

KITTY: I want this summer to be as pleasant and serene as possible.

ANNIE: Lil can take care of herself. She can. I think she can.

(Lights down on cabin, up on beach.)

LIL: *(As though concluding a description.)* . . . and to the left, that's the yacht basin. July 4th, they'll race, a hundred boats with spinnakers—it's really breathtaking.

EVA: You love it here, don't you?

LIL: It's my favorite place in all the world. I wish I'd found it sooner. This is only my fourth summer at the Cove.

EVA: Well, think of it this way. You have forty summers ahead of you. I think I'll head back to my cabin now. Thanks for inviting me.

LIL: It was awful for you, wasn't it? I'm sorry. The whole thing was just a terrible mistake.

EVA: I don't understand! I tried to be polite and sociable.

I tried to say the right things. I've never felt so left out in my life. I might as well have been speaking another language.

LIL: You were speaking another language.

EVA: I thought I had it figured out—no men, no husbands—then Rae started talking about her children.

LIL: Lesbians have children, too. Some lesbians do.

EVA: I feel like such a fool. Why didn't you just tell me?

LIL: I couldn't. I couldn't just say, all the women in this cove are lesbians—because I don't have the right to make that kind of announcement for them. They have to make the decision to tell that themselves and everybody doesn't make the same decision at the same time—it's a mess, that's what it is, a mess. It's hard on us and it's hard on you. I'm sorry.

EVA: They're probably up there right now, laughing at what an idiot I made of myself.

LIL: No, nobody wanted to hurt you or embarrass you, Eva. I should never have invited you tonight—but at the time I asked you, I thought you were one of us.

EVA: You what?

LIL: It was a logical assumption. Marge Eaton has never, in recorded history, rented a cabin in Bluefish Cove to a heterosexual.

EVA: Never?

LIL: Bluefish Cove has been a gay women's haven for thirty years or more. These cabins were built by two elderly "maiden ladies"—that's what the locals called them. One of them's still alive in a nursing home, up island. Couple of years ago, a bunch of us drove up to see her. Annie took some photographs of the yacht race on the Sound and Rae brought her a bouquet of lavender. She never did understand who we were or why we were there. She kept staring at us and twice she looked around as though there were someone standing behind her and she said, "Elizabeth, I believe we have some company." Elizabeth was her lover's name, I guess. I don't know what will happen to the Cove when the old lady dies.

EVA: You could buy it. You could all get together and buy it.

LIL: Maybe Sue will buy it. She has the money to do it. Or Kitty.

EVA: I can't believe that Kitty Cochrane . . .

LIL: Yeah, well, don't talk about it, huh? It really could hurt her career.

EVA: George always claimed that women's libbers were a bunch of . . .

LIL: Dykes? Not all—but some. After all, dykes are women, too. I'll call Marge tomorrow. I'll explain to her and maybe she'll cancel your rental contract.

EVA: I don't know where else to go. I need a friend now. I'd wanted it to be you.

LIL: I'm not a vampire, for heaven's sake. I don't go around pouncing on pretty women. I know how to be friends. But you won't be comfortable here, Eva. You're out of place.

EVA: I'm out of place everywhere, Lil. I'm out of place here, in my marriage, in my life. And I'm terrified to be alone. I've never been alone.

LIL: Everybody's alone, Eva, sooner or later—we do all the important things alone.

EVA: Not me.

LIL: You're alone getting born, giving birth, dying. Oh, people may be standing around you, watching you, but you do the thing alone. You fall in love alone. Yes, you do. It's not like dancing the tango, two people don't fall in love in lockstep. One falls first, one falls later and maybe one never falls at all. You say Kitty's book changed your life—it didn't. It might have given you some courage but you're the one who changed your life, Eva. You rented the cabin, you spoke to me on the beach, you asked me to be your friend—you're not nearly so dependent as you think you are, Eva. Wherever you go this summer, I expect you'll do just fine.

EVA: Those women in your cabin tonight, they all seem so independent. And you, you don't need anybody. I admire that. You're not afraid of anything. George says women can't get along without men. Ha. I wish he could have seen what I saw tonight.

LIL: Eva, forget what you saw tonight, huh? Go back to your cabin, get a good night's sleep and I'll call Marge for you in the morning. Go on. Oh Jesus, don't start crying.

EVA: I'm not crying! I'm mad. I'm scared. You don't want me here and I don't know where to go . . . you were going to be my friend . . .

LIL: Eva, I am your friend. Everything's going to be just fine, you'll see. Now, go on. It's freezing out here. Good night.

(*Reluctantly,* EVA *leaves.* LIL *watches, then turns and mounts stairs to cabin. Lights up in cabin.*)

ANNIE: Here she comes.

KITTY: Alone?

RAE: Well, hey there. We were getting worried about you.

LIL: Sorry. She was pretty upset. This has been a stinking party, hasn't it?

DONNA: It's early yet. We can still party.

SUE: *(Exiting bathroom.)* We're going home now, Donna.

DONNA: Why?

SUE: I'm tired. I'm menopausal!

DONNA: What a drag!

SUE: We'll see you on the beach tomorrow, okay? Donna?

DONNA: Lil, want to go sailing tomorrow?

SUE: Donna.

DONNA: You don't like to sail. It makes you seasick. Lil?

LIL: *(Her attention is toward the window.)* I'll take a raincheck, Donna.

SUE: Donna, come on.

DONNA: If you change your mind, Lil . . .

SUE: Donna. *(They exit.)*

ANNIE: I'd like to strangle that kid. What a cunt.

KITTY: Annie! Never use a woman's genitalia as a derogatory word. What kind of feminism is that?

ANNIE: Kitty, m'dear, it has been my experience that in any group of men you will find a number of pricks. And occasionally, mind you, occasionally, in a group of fine upstanding women like ourselves, you will find a cunt. Donna is one. She wants Lil's body.

KITTY: She's had Lil's body.

ANNIE: Well, apparently she didn't get enough of it.

LIL: How could she? Kitty was breaking down the motel room door.

KITTY: She isn't good for you.

LIL: Don't worry. I can't be bothered. I haven't the energy or time.

RAE: That's the most sensible thing I've heard you say since I've known you.

(KITTY *is preparing to leave.* RITA *follows suit.*)

KITTY: *(At door.)* All right, gang. I'm going into town at ten a.m. tomorrow morning. If you want anything, write it down and attach cash. Last year, I managed to lose a lot of money. "Oh, Kitty, pick up some aspirin for me, will you?" "Toothpaste, we're nearly out of toothpaste." "Tampax, I forgot to get Tampax." This year, Rita's keeping track and I'm going to bill you.

LIL: Once a nitpicker, always a nitpicker; becoming famous hasn't changed you one damn bit.

KITTY: Last chance. Night all.

RITA: Thank you. It was a lovely dinner, Rae.

(They exit. RAE *picks up the cups and stacks them in the sink.* LIL *stares out the window.*)

RAE: That Rita's got good manners. She's the only one who

said how good the meal was, the only one. The rest of you bums just took it for granted.

ANNIE: I never take you for granted, love, never. My life with you is a glorious adventure.

RAE: Are you making that up?

ANNIE: My nights are rich with mystery, my dreams breathless with expectation.

RAE: You read that somewhere!

ANNIE: I think I read it in a Kitty Cochrane book. *(RAE smacks her with dishtowel.)* On the other hand, maybe I overheard Lil saying that to Donna! *(Again, a smack.)*

ANNIE: *(Sees LIL.)* Are you okay, Lil?

LIL: Just tired.

ANNIE: Well, they told you to expect that, didn't they? Maybe you should take a nap in the afternoon.

LIL: I don't have time to take a nap.

ANNIE: Hey. *(She tries to comfort LIL but LIL brushes her off.)* You like her, huh? I know you. Do I know you or do I know you? I know you. You like her, huh? Huh? Am I right? You like her! Uh-huh!

LIL: *(Laughs.)* Kind of.

ANNIE: See there? Who knows you? I know you. Nobody knows you like I do. Right?

LIL: Right.

ANNIE: I love you, good buddy.

LIL: You said that earlier. Don't get mushy.

ANNIE: I know. My loving you is not enough. But just the same, I do. *(Calls to* RAE.*)* Come on, ol' lady, we're going home. Don Juan here is plumb wore out.

RAE: All right, all right, I'm just finishing up.

ANNIE: You need anything, Lil?

LIL: Yeah. Time.

ANNIE: You really like her.

LIL: She needs somebody. So do I.

ANNIE: Well then?

LIL: No. Wouldn't work.

ANNIE: Never say never.

LIL: She's straight.

ANNIE: Maybe she is and maybe she isn't.

LIL: She is.

ANNIE: I thought Rae was, too. Married lady with chubby babies hanging on her skirt. Then she attacked me.

LIL: It's not the same thing. You could offer her a life together.

ANNIE: You don't know yet what you could offer her—it's not the quantity of time, Lil, it's the quality—and you've got lots of quality, my friend.

LIL: You know, the one thing I've always had going for me is I know who I am. I know who I am, what I am, and what I'm capable of doing. Most of the time, I actually know what I want.

ANNIE: And?

LIL: She doesn't. She doesn't know a thing about herself. I don't make brass sculptures that last forever. I never wrote a book or had a baby. I'd like to pass something on.

RAE: *(To ANNIE.)* Okay, hot shot, let's go.

ANNIE: We'll see you in the morning?

LIL: Thanks, both of you.

RAE: When you get to feeling better, you can cook for us and wash our dishes.

LIL: That's a deal.

ANNIE: Get some sleep, will you?

LIL: I'll try. I get tired but my mind won't stop. I don't want to waste time sleeping.

ANNIE: I bet you could work up a terrific erotic dream tonight. Now, I don't consider that a waste of time!

LIL: *(Grins.)* You may be right about that.

ANNIE: Do I know you, huh?

LIL: Will you get outta here? *(They exit. LIL straightens up, unmakes the bed, sits on it, despondent. To herself.)* It isn't fair. *(She examines ANNIE's sculpture on table, replaces it, lights a cigarette, then hurls the ashtray on the floor.)* God-dammit. *(She bursts into tears and races into the bathroom.)*

(Lights slowly down on cabin, up on beach. A passage of time. EVA, wrapped in jacket and shivering against the sea breeze, enters. She looks up at the cabin and begins to mount the stairs. LIL, coming out of the bathroom, is startled by the knock.)

LIL: Who is it?

EVA: I'm too upset to sleep.

LIL: *(Not going to door.)* It's late, Eva. I'm very tired.

EVA: But I need to talk.

LIL: *(Reluctantly coming to door.)* We'll talk tomorrow. Life doesn't look so damned dramatic in the sunlight.

EVA: Have you been crying? Your face is swollen.

LIL: Naw. Catching a cold or something.

EVA: Your eyes are puffy.

LIL: Probably an allergic reaction to the sun. I stayed on the beach too long this afternoon.

EVA: I warned you. Bet your shoulders are blistered.

LIL: No, they're fine.

(EVA *touches* LIL's *shoulder;* LIL *winces.)*

EVA: See? You ought to put something on them. You have some Noxema?

LIL: No, Eva. I'm just fine. I'm terrific, wonderful. Good night.

EVA: It gets cold here at night, doesn't it? *(She shivers visibly.)* That sea breeze. . . .

LIL: All right, Eva, but not for long. I've got to get some sleep.

(She lets her in. LIL keeps her distance. EVA sits awk-wardly.)

EVA: I used to talk to my little boy, Lenny, late at night like this. I'd sit by his bed and talk and he'd listen to me. He lived to be six years old. I taught him to read—he loved to read. He'd read to me out loud. I'd never been much of a reader myself, until Lenny came along. Then I started going to the library and bookstores to get books for him—and I'd pick up something for myself. In a way, you could say Lenny taught me to read. I think George thought he was somehow responsible for Lenny's heart. George thinks he's responsible for everything. He's not a mean man, he's just set in his ways. My mother wanted me to marry an adventurer—she was always dreaming about adventures. Going places no one else had gone, doing things no one had done —she never went anywhere herself, of course, it all happened in her mind. She wanted me to have adventures for her. And I haven't had a one. . . .

LIL: Oh, I'm sure you have, Eva. Coming to the party tonight was a kind of adventure, wasn't it? Maybe not a pleasant one, but—

EVA: I bet you have adventures all the time.

LIL: Don't make a heroine out of me, Eva.

EVA: But I admire you.

LIL: I've done a whole lot of things in my life which were not in the least bit admirable. Ask Kitty Cochrane, she'll give you an earful.

EVA: Were you and Kitty . . .

LIL: For a while.

EVA: But now, you're not . . .

LIL: It's not a time for me to make commitments. I was never much for making commitments, anyway.

EVA: How did you know you were?

LIL: *(Challenging her.)* What?

EVA: *(Forcing herself to say it.)* Gay.

LIL: I fell in love with a woman. *(Snaps.)* What is this, twenty questions?

EVA: I'm sorry—I just don't know anything about it and—

LIL: Okay. I knew very early, some people do. I knew when I couldn't take my eyes off my high school English teacher, when my knees quivered every time my chemistry lab partner brushed her elbow against mine. When I could hardly wait for double dates to end so my girlfriend and I could cuddle in her bed together and demonstrate to one another what the boys had done to us. I knew it didn't mean a thing to her—that when I touched her, she was pretending that I was a boy. But I wasn't pretending. She was the real thing for me. I didn't know there were so many others like me until I got to college and met Annie. Annie swears that she was born gay. She was playing doctor with little girls in kindergarten. She's never had the slightest heterosexual tendency.

EVA: So, it was you and Annie?

LIL: Oh, goodness, no. Never. Annie and I are best buddies. It was Annie who showed me the gay bars and restaurants, the gay resort areas—we gays are kind of like the hobbits—no matter how repressive earthlings get, we continue to thrive in Middle Earth. We're survivors. We straddle both worlds and try to keep our balance.

EVA: Kitty Cochrane's book says you can be bisexual. She says it's the most natural way to be.

LIL: *(Sardonically.)* She does, huh?

EVA: I'd really never thought about that before.

LIL: *(Knowing what is coming.)* Well, Kitty also claims a mature person should not expect their partner to remain monogamous, that jealousy is an immature response. And I'm here to tell you that what Kitty says and what Kitty does are not the same thing. Kitty is a very possessive lady.

EVA: You don't like her, do you? You're always putting her down.

LIL: Like Kitty? I adore Kitty. She's my good friend. I might poke a little fun at Dr. Kitty Cochrane, feminist soothsayer, but that's just a mask she wears. The real Kitty is an old-time friend of mine. We've been through a lot together. Kitty's all right. I can count on Kitty to come through.

EVA: Lil, were you ever attracted to a man?

LIL: Are you writing a book or what? It's after midnight!

EVA: *(Flustered.)* No, I'm just trying to . . .

LIL: *(Challenging.)* To *what?*

EVA: *(Quietly.)* To understand. You think I'm boring, don't you?

LIL: No. . . .

EVA: Just another runaway housewife.

LIL: I don't think you're boring, Eva. You're lonely, vulnerable, curious—and that combination scares the hell out of me. *(LIL smiles at EVA.)*

EVA: *(Shyly.)* I thought about you ever since I saw you on

the beach today—at the party tonight, I could feel you watching me. I thought I could. *(LIL shrugs, admitting it.)* I sensed something was happening between us, I mean, I've never felt this kind of thing with a woman and I didn't know how to . . . I don't know how to . . . I mean, I've never . . . I wasn't even sure, I'm not sure . . . *(LIL begins to grin, watching EVA stammer through this.) (Quietly smiling.)* Are you just going to let me stand here and make a fool out of myself?

LIL: I'm not a curiosity, Eva. I'm not an experiment, not an adventure. On the other hand, I have never, repeat *never*, gone shopping with anybody for matching sheets and drapes at Bloomingdale's.

EVA: I understand.

LIL: *(Touching her face.)* Do you?

EVA: *(Bravely.)* I'm not as naive as you think I am.

LIL: You're not? *(LIL touches EVA seductively.)*

EVA: All right, I am.

LIL: Uh-huh. *(She guides EVA toward door.)* Go home, Eva. It's late, I'm tired, I'll see you on the beach tomorrow. We'll spend the afternoon together on the beach, all right? *(She touches EVA's lips with her fingers. Sighs.)* My mother must have told me fifty times, never kiss on the first date.

EVA: You're a puritan.

LIL: No, but my mother is. This is the first time I've ever taken her advice. Goodnight. *(EVA starts to descend stairs, looks back.)* Goodnight, Eva.

(LIL smiles as EVA *exits, but the smile fades to anxiety as)*

BLACKOUT

ACT TWO

(Midsummer now. KITTY, RITA, RAE and DONNA are sunbathing on the beach. DONNA wears her useless sandals and a giant beach hat and the smallest possible bikini. RAE, KITTY and RITA wear ordinary bathing suits and are passing around a thermos of martinis. ANNIE, in ragged cutoffs and a shirt with the sleeves ripped out of it, is barefooted on the rock, fishing. SUE is with her. DONNA struts back and forth, displaying her body and glancing up at the cabin with irritation.)

DONNA: Don't they ever get out of bed?

RAE: Why don't you mind your own business?

DONNA: Well, they can't be doing it all the time. It's physically impossible.

RITA: Kitty says women are capable of many multiple orgasms. Men aren't but women are.

DONNA: Well, I think it's perverted. We've hardly seen Lil all summer.

RAE: It's Lil's summer. If she wants to spend it in bed, let her.

DONNA: Well, it isn't fair.

KITTY: You'd think it was fair enough if you were the one in bed with her. *(SUE turns and catches KITTY's eye. To SUE.)* Sorry.

    (DONNA climbs partway up the stairs, looking. SUE watches her.)

ANNIE: *(To SUE.)* You deserve better than that, Sue.

SUE: Do I?

ANNIE: Yes. She uses you.

SUE: They all do. She's not the first pretty young thing I've kept. I don't expect she'll be the last.

ANNIE: You're a nice lady. You don't have to buy love.

SUE: I have never known, in fact, who loved me and who loved my bankbook—except with this one. I don't have to lie awake nights saying to myself, "But she said this," or, "She did this," and, "Maybe that does mean she loves me"—with Donna, I know exactly where I stand. *(Lightly.)* It hurts less that way, Annie.

KITTY: *(Calling to* DONNA.*)* Come down from there, leave her alone.

DONNA: None of you are concerned about Lil. *(She comes down.)* You don't care whether you see her this summer or not. You don't care if you ever see her again.

RAE: Of course we care.

DONNA: Any day could be her last.

KITTY: Oh, don't be so dramatic, Donna. People in Lil's condition just don't keel over suddenly. She'll have adequate warning and so will we.

RAE: I saw them walking on the beach this morning. Lil looked fine, her color's good. And I don't know when I've seen her look so happy.

RITA: I saw Eva in the supermarket. She looks good, too. She was all excited about moving into Lil's apartment in the city—she said they'd signed a lease to take the cabin again next summer.

KITTY: She said what?

RAE: She hasn't told her!

KITTY: Why didn't you tell me that?

RITA: I told you I saw her.

KITTY: But you didn't tell me that.

RITA: You were writing. I didn't want to break your concentration.

RAE: Annie! *(ANNIE leaps from rock to shore, turns to offer SUE a hand.)*

ANNIE: Yeah. I don't know what it is Lil does to catch fish off this rock but I don't seem to have any luck at all.

RAE: Did you know that Lil hasn't told Eva?

ANNIE: Hasn't told her what? *(Pauses, realizes.)* She hasn't?

KITTY: I understand it but I'm not happy about it. Lil's going through denial. It's natural—but in these circumstances—

ANNIE: I wouldn't tell her, either.

DONNA: I would—it would be so—romantic. Like Camille.

SUE: Will you shut up?

ANNIE: *(To SUE.)* Thank you. That's a step in the right direction, Sue.

RAE: But it isn't right, not to tell her. Eva ought to know.

ANNIE: As long as Lil feels good, I don't see why she has to tell her. Lil doesn't want to be looked on as a dying woman, for Christ's sake. Would you? She's in love, she feels wonderful, she wants to live. Leave her alone.

DONNA: You'd think she'd want to spend her last days with her friends. She just met Eva—she's known us for years.

ANNIE: *(To SUE.)* Will you do something about that brat before I drown her?

DONNA: I don't have to take that from you. I don't have to stand here and be insulted by a bunch of dykes.

ANNIE: Oh, and what are you, sweetheart, chopped liver?

DONNA: I'm bisexual. Or I could be if I wanted to. When we took that cruise to St. John's last year, I could have had every man on shipboard, couldn't I, Sue?

SUE: To tell the truth, dear, I thought you did.

DONNA: Well, I didn't! But nobody could blame me if I had. I certainly don't get any at home!

RAE: Donna!

DONNA: *(To ANNIE.)* You don't care about Lil. You're just going to let her stay up in that cabin with that stranger all summer long. She's going to die and we'll never see her again and you don't care. I'm going back to the cabin, Sue. *(She hobbles off.)* Sue? I'm going back to the cabin, aren't you coming? *(No answer.)* Sue!

SUE: *(Not moving.)* No. You're a big girl, Donna. You can get here to there alone. *(DONNA is stunned.)* Go on. *(DONNA, puzzled and disgruntled, hobbles off.)*

ANNIE: *(To* SUE.*)* Good girl.

SUE: She's spoiled rotten. And I'm the one who spoiled her. She was a perfectly ordinary little girl from Brooklyn when I met her. Oh, she'd gone to modeling school but she worked as a trainee on the Information Desk at Bloomingdale's. I was looking for the sale in Sportswear and she directed me first to Home Furnishings and then to Men's Outerwear and finally to Lingerie. She had a wonderful sense of humor about her inefficiency and never once apologized for sending me on wild goose chases all over the store. Donna was not always what she is now. I played a part in creating the monster. And like Dr. Frankenstein, I am somewhat reluctant to release my creation on the world.

(Lights dim on beach, up in cabin. EVA is sitting on the unmade bed. She has a pad of paper in her lap; she is making a list. LIL is not in sight.)

EVA: How big is your dining room?

LIL: *(Sticking her head out the bathroom door, washing her face.)* What?

EVA: Your dining room?

LIL: *Our* dining room.

EVA: How big is it?

LIL: *(Coming out, still scrubbing her face.)* It's very tiny. Actually, it's not a dining room, it's an alcove. It's, oh, I don't know, about like—I don't know, honey, it's little.

EVA: Will it hold an oak table and six bentwood chairs?

LIL: Sweetheart, this is a very small apartment.

EVA: But I have so much gorgeous furniture. Do I have to leave it all for George? *(LIL goes back to bathroom.)* We can get a bigger apartment.

LIL: *(Returning.)* Honey, I can afford *this* apartment.

EVA: Well, I can get a job. Some kind of job. Can't I? Do you want me to work?

LIL: *(From bathroom.)* It's not what I want, Eva, it's what *you* want. What do you want? *(LIL exits the bathroom, finished.)* What do you want?

EVA: I wish you'd stop asking me that.

LIL: I don't want you to do anything to please me. Just please yourself.

EVA: But I don't know what I want. Except you. I want you. Always.

LIL: *(Efficiently.)* It may come as a big surprise to you, my darling, but there is more to life than— *(EVA kisses her lightly, seductively, then moves away.)* —uhhhh. *(LIL follows. The following dialogue occurs during a slow-moving chase—EVA seducing, LIL reaching out, EVA moving away. It's a lovers' dance.)*

EVA: More to life than what?

LIL: Don't listen to me. I don't know what I'm talking about.

EVA: More to life than sex?

LIL: Some people say that but they lie. It's a pack of lies.

EVA: You mean love does make the world go round?

LIL: Oh, definitely.

EVA: Resolves all problems?

LIL: Absolutely.

EVA: Love conquers all?

LIL: No doubt about it.

EVA: My mother used to tell me, "Marry a rich man. Love doesn't pay the rent."

LIL: Your mother is a callous woman.

EVA: Will a six-foot couch fit in your living room?

LIL: *Our* living room.

EVA: Will it?

LIL: Honey, a six-foot person will hardly fit in that living room.

EVA: What am I supposed to do with all my furniture?

LIL: Sell it, store it, give it to George, give it to your mother, give it to the Salvation Army, burn it, just stop talking about it, put that damn list away and come here.

EVA: My mother always told me to plan for the future.

LIL: I can see your mother and I are not going to get along.

EVA: We have so much future to plan for, Lil—so many years together, so many things to do—do you ski?

LIL: Do I ski? I was the college downhill champion.

EVA: I'm the snowplow queen myself. You can follow my trail by the sitzmarks. But I love it. Imagine riding beside you in a chairlift. I've always had a fantasy about making love in a chairlift. Everybody on the mountain's craning their necks looking but they can't get to me and my lover, we're isolated, out of reach, oblivious to their stares and shouts, caught in the frenzy of our insatiable desire. Want to try that?

LIL: Nope. You might have gotten away with doing that with George but if you and I tried it, there'd be a sheriff waiting on the platform.

EVA: I never did it with George. George was never even in that fantasy.

LIL: But it was a man in the fantasy.

EVA: Well, I didn't know any better. Let's go to Switzerland and ski the Alps. And Spain. You want to go to Spain? I've never been to Spain.

LIL: Nope. I don't want to go to Spain. They throw homosexuals in jail in Spain. They'll take one look at the way my knees quiver when you look at me and they'll put me in the hoosegow and throw away the key. Let's go to Amsterdam. We can get married in Amsterdam.

EVA: Really?

LIL: Yep, we're nice and legal there, just like ordinary folks. Want to marry me?

EVA: Ah, you say that to all your girls.

LIL: I never said it before in my whole life. Girl-Scout's honor. It might make your mother happy. She sounds like the kind of woman who doesn't want you to live in sin.

EVA: What am I going to tell her?

LIL: That you've left George.

EVA: I've already told her that. I called her the night I did it. She was hysterical for twenty minutes but she got over it. She and George never got along. I'm sure she's already called her friends to elicit names of suitable eligible men.

LIL: Tell her you have a roommate.

EVA: What if I tell her the truth?

LIL: Don't.

EVA: Why not?

LIL: Does she vote a liberal ticket? Did she march for civil rights? Did she protest the war in Viet Nam? Did she boycott grapes and support the draft evaders?

EVA: No.

LIL: Don't tell her then. It's ten to one she'll disown you as a pervert.

EVA: She wouldn't.

LIL: Mine did. Just say you have a roommate and keep your mouth shut. Unless, of course, you get off on verbal flagellation and suicide threats.

EVA: I don't want to have to lie to my mother. I've never lied to my mother.

LIL: Everybody has lied to their mother.

EVA: Well, not about anything important.

LIL: Annie's mother won't allow Rae in the house. Sue's brothers won't allow her to visit her nieces and nephews. Rita was trained to be a teacher, you know, junior high school math. Her father called the school board and reported her. My mother feigned a suicide attempt and then had a nervous breakdown. Her shrink finally convinced her that my sexuality was not her fault and now she has disowned me. She wipes her hands of me, she says. She says I have faulty genes and I'm a malicious pervert. I keep reading stories in the gay press about how eighteen-year-olds announce it to their families over Christmas dinner and everybody hugs each other and it's all hunky-dory. Well, maybe that happens to eighteen-year-olds but it's never happened to anybody I know. The only one I know who has remained unscathed by their family is Kitty Cochrane—and that's because she has remained safely inside the closet.

EVA: I don't want to lose my family—but I don't want to lie to them, either. I want them to share my happiness. I want them to know you and love you. . . .

LIL: Don't count on it, Eva. Don't tell them unless you're prepared to lose them. I don't think you should tell them anything at all, not yet. I mean, we're very new, you and me, and what if you change your mind, what if something happens—next year this time you could be married to some upstanding dentist in Westchester.

EVA: Lil! You don't mean that.

LIL: Why not?

EVA: I love you! This may have started out to be a summer fling but it's much more than that now—what's the matter with you?

LIL: I'm trying to be realistic, Eva. Things change, people change.

EVA: But you love me—you said you love me. Or is that just part of the game, part of the malicious perversion?

LIL: *(Embraces* EVA.*)* I love you more than I have ever loved anyone. For the first time in my life, I understand why knights rode miles to slay a dragon for their lady's hand.

EVA: *(Half-crying, half-laughing.)* Lil.

LIL: And all those songs with "moon" and "June" and "croon," I thought they were pretty silly. Now, I'm whistling those tunes in the shower. Remember that song, "You're My Everything"? I used to hear that and say to myself, now what the hell does that mean, "You're my everything"? Nobody's anybody's everything. I was wrong.

EVA: Lil?

LIL: Yes, angel?

EVA: Are you ashamed of me? Do I embarrass you?

LIL: What?

EVA: You don't see your friends any more. Since I've been living here, you don't ever ask them over. I see them on the path and they ask how you are—they look at me funny as though I've taken you away from them.

LIL: I'd rather be alone with you.

EVA: At first I thought they didn't like me. And maybe you

were embarrassed about me. That first party—it was awful. I know I made a bad impression.

LIL: Eva—I'm proud of you.

EVA: Do you know what tomorrow is?

LIL: Saturday?

EVA: It's our first anniversary. One month.

LIL: Oh, dear. If you cry because I forgot our first anniversary. . . .

EVA: Let's celebrate tomorrow night.

LIL: All right.

EVA: Invite your friends?

LIL: Not just the two of us?

EVA: We can't live in a vacuum forever. Besides, I want to show off. I want all your friends to see how much in love we are. I'm not such a dummy as they thought.

LIL: All right, you asked for it! *(She opens the door, runs partway down the steps.)* Hey gang! Hey, down there! We're throwing a beach party tomorrow night—steamed clams and crabs and lobsters! It's our first anniversary! Bring your own booze—

(The lights fade on the cabin and we hear the sound of

a transistor radio on the beach. It's the night of the party, the beach is lit by moonlight. DONNA, SUE, RITA *and* KITTY *go to the edges of the stage, collecting driftwood for the fire.* LIL *joins* ANNIE *on the beach—they are laying the firewood.* RAE *climbs the stairs to help* EVA *prepare the party food in the cabin kitchen.)*

LIL: Next year I'm going to buy some of that fire-starter, that stuff in cans. Trying to light a fire this big with drift and matches is an exercise in frustration.

ANNIE: I thought you were a Girl Scout, you got a merit badge in beach survival.

LIL: I did, I did, but I think I must have cheated—damned if I can remember how I did it.

ANNIE: You probably didn't do it at all. You charmed some little redhead into doing it for you.

LIL: That's not unlikely. That's how I passed Home Economics. Priscilla Miller, who could sew a seam straight as a ruler and fry an egg without breaking the yoke, lives forever in my grateful heart. *(She stands up, breathes the sea air.)* Annie, I feel terrific. I never felt so good in my whole life.

ANNIE: I'm glad, Lil. I'm happy for you. For both of you.

LIL: Doctors aren't infallible, you know. Sometimes these things just stop—the condition arrests itself, recedes, it goes away. When I was going to the clinic for chemotherapy, I met this woman whose tumor'd just stopped, disappeared, seventeen years ago. Then it came back—but she had a seventeen-year reprieve. It happens. She said she knew she couldn't die because she had to raise three kids—so she didn't die. And for seventeen years, until her kids were grown, she felt fine. It's all in having something to live for, Annie. I have Eva to live for now.

ANNIE: I've known you for a long time, Lil, and I don't think I've ever seen you in love before. Not like this.

LIL: It's never been like this. I didn't know it could be like this. Is it like this for you and Rae?

ANNIE: Well, probably not exactly—well, yes, I guess so. I mean, we've kind of passed that stage where we can't keep our hands off each other, thank goodness. You mellow out after a while, you know.

LIL: You mean the honeymoon ends.

ANNIE: Yeah—but that's when the good stuff starts.

LIL: Couldn't be any better than this. In ten years, we'll match notes, okay?

ANNIE: You haven't told Eva, have you?

LIL: She asked about the scar. I told her I had a hysterectomy. Which is true. She doesn't need to know any more than that— what more is there? I feel terrific. They told me I'd start having short-term pain. I haven't felt a thing. I'm telling you, Annie, it's gone. I know it is.

(DONNA approaches LIL with an armful of firewood.)

DONNA: This is getting my shirt all dirty. *(LIL takes the wood, DONNA brushes at her shirt.)*

LIL: Come on gang, keep the driftwood coming.

SUE: *(Depositing her load and collapsing on the beach.)* Enough already!

RAE: *(Out the cabin door.)* Hey, we could use some help up here!

SUE: I volunteer! Anything to get out of this! *(She gratefully climbs the steps.)*

KITTY: *(Dumping driftwood.)* I really think this is enough, Lil. We're cooking seafood, not signalling for rescue.

LIL: One more. One more armful.

KITTY: You overdo, Lil. You always overdo.

(RITA is staggering up with her armload.)

RITA: *(To KITTY.)* Is this it?

KITTY: She says one more. *(Contemplates RITA's pile.)* I'll take half of this, she'll never know the difference.

(Lights down on beach, up in cabin.)

SUE: *(Peering in pot.)* Jesus, that thing's alive!

RAE: They're all alive. That's how you cook them, alive.

SUE: Well, I know that, but I thought you drugged them or something first.

RAE: Nope. Right into the fire, alive.

SUE: I wish I hadn't seen it. It looked directly at me.

EVA: I take it you don't cook.

SUE: Only under duress. If push comes to shove, I can put a TV dinner in the oven.

EVA: Donna does the cooking?

SUE: Are you kidding? In the city, the cook does the cooking. When we travel, the hotel does the cooking and out here, we eat two meals a day at Molly Pitcher's.

RAE: Can you count to eight? Then count out the paper napkins, forks, spoons, glasses, paper plates—put them in that box and carry them downstairs. *(SUE grimaces and proceeds to do so.)*

EVA: *(To SUE.)* You travel all year round from place to place?

SUE: All my life. When I was growing up, it was Bar Harbor in the summer, a Massachusetts girls' school in the fall, Christmas in London, back to school for the winter, spring in Paris or Switzerland, back to Bar Harbor. There was a townhouse in the city we called home—my father lived there most of the time but the rest of us wafted in and out, on our way to somewhere else.

EVA: That's the kind of life my mother always said she wished that she could give me.

SUE: It was a nightmare.

EVA: I never went away to school. I went to a local college and lived at home. When George and I first married, we lived with his family for a year before we bought a place of our own. My mother was never crazy about George. She said that he was dull. If Lil were male, my mother would approve her as the perfect choice. We're going to travel, we're going to ski the Alps and Lil wants to take me to Amsterdam. Did you know you can get married in Amsterdam?

SUE: I thought you could get married anywhere.

EVA: A man and woman can get married anywhere. I mean Lil and me. We could get married in Amsterdam.

RAE: Whatever for?

EVA: Well, it would be kind of romantic.

SUE: For god's sake, don't tell Donna about it. She'd marry me, divorce me and wipe me out.

EVA: Oh, no she wouldn't.

RAE: Oh, yes she would.

EVA: Well, I'm glad I married George—I spent twelve years with him. If I'd just lived with him, if I didn't have a marriage contract, I wouldn't get a thing.

RAE: You may not get a thing. I didn't. Not one red cent. I put him through school, raised two kids, kept his house—now if he'd left me, I'd have had him by the short hairs. But I left him, see, and I left him for a woman. The only way he'd agree to let me keep the kids was if I forfeited my suit for child support. Annie's putting my kids through college.

EVA: But George and I bought that house together, we furnished it together, he made investments in the market for both of us.

RAE: In your name?

EVA: I don't know. George took care of those things.

RAE: Did he beat you up?

EVA: No!

RAE: Have a mistress?

EVA: Not that I know of—maybe.

RAE: Unless you can prove abuse or adultery, you're probably out of luck, sweetheart. At least in this state. You left him. And for heaven's sake, don't ever let him know you left him for a woman. Zilch. You'll get zilch.

EVA: But I never had to earn a living. George made good

money. I don't know how to be anything but a housewife.

RAE: Me, either. And I'm good at it. I like to make a home, I like to shop, cook, clean. When my kids act up or Annie and I have a fight, I like to get down on my knees with a scrub-brush and wash that kitchen floor until it squeaks. It's a blasphemous thing to say in this age of Kitty Cochrane feminism, but I like creating an environment that's warm and pretty for the people I love.

EVA: Do your kids understand—about you and Annie?

RAE: Oh, we worried ourselves sick about that. We practiced just how we were going to tell the kids. Before we got up the courage to do it, they told us. They'd known it all along. My daughter went through a bad period about it when she was thirteen, fourteen—you know girls that age can't stand to be the least bit different—having a lesbian mother was an embarrassment, I guess. Even now, I'm not as close to her as I'd like to be—we get along all right but something's missing between us. My boy, it didn't phase him. He's a good kid, hair down to his ass but a mother can't have everything. *(She changes the subject abruptly.)* Okay, Eva, grab that pot, will you? And can you carry this box, too? Be careful with that, hold it upright.

EVA: *(Looking in box.)* What is it?

RAE: Get your nose out of there. It's a surprise.

EVA: It's a cake!

SUE: *(Looking.)* "Happy Number One. And Many More."

RAE: *And many more.*

EVA: Well, I should hope so. It's only a month. I expect us to stay together until we're ninety.

(They gather up the boxes and bags and start downstairs as the lights dim in the cabin and come up on beach. DONNA is sitting on the stairs, watching. The others have finished preparing the fire.)

ANNIE: Fire's going good.

DONNA: At last.

LIL: You haven't done a thing to help.

DONNA: I did so. I carried wood.

SUE: *(Calls from above.)* Donna! I could use some help with this.

DONNA: *(Mimicking.)* "Donna," "Donna."

ANNIE: Give her a break, will you? She's damned nice to you. Show some appreciation.

DONNA: She doesn't want me to be nice to her, don't you know that? If I were nice to her, she'd drop me in a minute. *(DONNA goes to help.)*

ANNIE: *(To KITTY.)* You understand that?

KITTY: Yes.

ANNIE: You would.

KITTY: *(As though from a textbook.)* Sue lacks self-esteem so she asks Donna to reinforce that she, Sue, is, in fact, not worthy of receiving love. If Donna were to demonstrate affection for Sue, Sue would feel betrayed and her emotional dependence on Donna would no doubt cease. It's a classic interaction between neurotics—the symptoms vary from battering to emotional flagellation. It is not infrequently found in parent/child and employer/employee relationships as well as those of mates. In the case of Donna and Sue, Donna, as the flagellator, also experiences guilt because she does, in fact, harbor affection for Sue but she senses, accurately, that to demonstrate that affection would jeopardize the game on which their relationship is based. It is this guilt which causes Donna to act promiscuously as in the case of Lil where Donna wishes Lil to punish her in the same way Donna has punished Sue.

LIL: *(To* ANNIE.*)* I'm sorry you asked that.

ANNIE: Not as sorry as I am.

RITA: *(Who has been following this carefully.)* You mean that Donna wants Lil to beat her up?

KITTY: Emotionally, dear, emotionally.

RITA: Because she feels guilty because she's so nasty to Sue.

KITTY: That's right.

RITA: Well, why *is* she so nasty to Sue? *(KITTY opens her mouth to explain. ANNIE stops her.)*

ANNIE: Don't you say that again. I got a headache the first time. *(To RITA.)* Donna is nasty to Sue because Sue's a sap and Donna's a cunt. *(She dares KITTY to challenge that.)*

KITTY: Well, I suppose that's another way of putting it.

(The others arrive on the beach and unload beside the fire.)

LIL: Where's the beer? You forgot the beer!

RAE: I set it on the counter. The big red cooler. I thought you had it, Sue.

SUE: I thought Donna got it.

DONNA: I only carried what you handed to me, Sue. I'm not a mind reader.

EVA: I'll go back up.

LIL: No, I'll go, honey.

ANNIE: Oh, no you don't. I'll go.

KITTY: *(To LIL.)* Let Annie go. That cooler's heavy.

LIL: *(Challenging her.)* So what?

KITTY: Lil. Let Annie go.

LIL: No. I said I'm going.

ANNIE: *(Pushing her aside gently.)* Out of the way, pal.

LIL: *(Seizing her.)* I said I'm going. *(Meanwhile, EVA is completely bewildered by all this.)*

DONNA: *(Grabbing LIL.)* Listen to Kitty, she's your doctor.

LIL: She's not my doctor. There's nothing wrong with me! Let me go, Annie. *(ANNIE looks at KITTY.)* Don't do this to me, Kitty.

KITTY: *(To ANNIE.)* Let her go. *(LIL races up the stairs.)*

EVA: What was that about?

RAE: Rita? Give me a hand here, will you? Push back those coals, Annie, so we can dump the clams in.

EVA: *(To RAE.)* What happened?

RAE: *(Pats EVA's hand.)* Nothing, honey, nothing happened. Sue?

SUE: Don't you ask me to pick up one of those evil-looking critters.

EVA: *(Persistent.)* Something happened but I didn't understand.

ANNIE: *(To KITTY.)* She swears she feels fine.

KITTY: Maybe she does.

ANNIE: She says being in love has cured her.

KITTY: Oh, Annie, I hope that's true. I really want to believe in miracles—I want a miracle for her.

(LIL *appears at the top of the stairs with the cooler. She lifts it over her head and, showing off, descends the stairs.*)

ANNIE: Jesus, Lil!

LIL: I'm an Amazon! I can lift bull elephants above my head. I can slay dragons to win my lady's hand. *(ANNIE starts to help her.)* Don't, Annie, you'll upset my balance. *(ANNIE stops. They all watch breathlessly as* LIL *successfully completes the steps and presents the cooler at* EVA's *feet.)* Voila! *(She takes a deep bow. To* ANNIE.*)* See? *(To* KITTY.*)* Now get the hell off my back.

RITA: She's only trying to help you!

LIL: I don't need her help. *(But at that moment the abdominal pain strikes and bends her double.)*

ANNIE: Lil!

LIL: Don't touch me! I'm all right! I'm going to be all right! *(It hits her again.)* Eva! *(EVA, bewildered, frightened, reaches out to* LIL.*)* I'm going to be fine, Eva. It's nothing, really. I'm going to be just fine. *(It hits again.)*

KITTY: *(To* ANNIE.*)* Help me get her up the stairs. *(They move to do so.)*

EVA: What's wrong? What's the matter with her? Lil?

KITTY: *(To* ANNIE.*)* You get her shoulders. *(As they straighten her up,* LIL *cries with pain.)*

ANNIE: Take it easy, pal, we got you.

EVA: What's wrong? What are you doing to her?

LIL: Eva!

KITTY: Sorry, Eva, out of the way.

EVA: Lil!

(As they carry LIL *upstairs, the lights fade on the beach. There is a complete blackout and when the lights come up, one week has passed. On the stage is an open overnight case.* KITTY *and* LIL's *voices come from the bathroom.)*

KITTY: *(From bathroom.)* Lil, listen to me.

LIL: *(From bathroom.)* You're wasting your breath, Kitty.

KITTY: *(From bathroom.)* Lil, you're stubborn as a mule.

(During this, ANNIE *comes out of closet where she has been hanging up* LIL's *nightshirt. She returns to open overnight bag and continues to unpack. She takes out robe and*

hangs it in closet, returns to take out slippers, toothpaste, etc.)

LIL: *(From bathroom.)* Don't lecture me, Kitty.

KITTY: *(From bathroom.)* Put on your bathrobe. *(Out door, to ANNIE.)* Where's her robe? *(ANNIE hands it to KITTY.)*

LIL: *(From bathroom.)* Go to hell.

KITTY: *(In bathroom.)* Put it on. You just got out of the hospital, for Christ's sake, Lil. You're going to lie down and rest if I have to tie you to the bed. *(KITTY, irritated, exits bathroom. To ANNIE.)* Can't you talk some sense into her.

ANNIE: I'm her best friend, not her keeper.

KITTY: She wants to go fishing.

LIL: *(From bathroom, hollers.)* I feel fine!

ANNIE: *(To KITTY about overnight bag.)* I'm unpacking this.

KITTY: *(Irritated.)* I see you are.

ANNIE: She said to unpack it.

LIL: *(Entering, wearing robe halfheartedly.)* I'm not going back to the hospital, Kitty.

(ANNIE unpacks cigarettes from bag and puts them tentatively on counter. KITTY reaches for them but LIL slaps her hand protectively across them.)

KITTY: You're self-destructive.

LIL: My lungs are fine. My lungs have always been fine. Pink and healthy as a baby's. *(LIL reaches for a drink.)* My liver's fine, too.

KITTY: Lie down, Lil. Please.

LIL: Stop trying to turn me into an invalid!

KITTY: Just *walked* out of the hospital. *Walked* out.

LIL: I'm an adult human being. I have a few civil rights left.

KITTY: Lil, you're not being reasonable.

LIL: Fuck reasonable! This is my body, my life. I'll decide what's going to happen to me.

ANNIE: Lil . . .

LIL: *(To* ANNIE.*)* Don't you start on me. You're supposed to be on *my* side.

KITTY: There are no sides. You need surgery.

LIL: Sure. I need surgery this month and I'll need it again next month and again in two months—you know the statistics, Kitty.

KITTY: It will prolong your life, Lil.

LIL: In a hospital bed? No thanks.

ANNIE: You could let them try the cobalt again. . . .

KITTY: You responded very well to chemotherapy last spring.

LIL: For six weeks I was nauseated all day, my hair started falling out, I broke out in blotches, I was so weak I could hardly get from one room to another—Annie and Rae were waiting on me day and night. . . .

ANNIE: We didn't mind!

LIL: I mind!

KITTY: But the treatments helped. You felt wonderful until last week on the beach. . . .

LIL: And I feel fine again now. Without operations, without treatments, I feel fine.

KITTY: Bullshit, Lil.

LIL: They've already got my ovaries, uterus, tubes—if I'm going, I'm going with my hair, guts, breasts, whatever I've got left. I'm going as a person, not a patient. I'm going wanting to live, not wishing I were dead.

KITTY: You are stubborn and bullheaded—and you won't let anybody help you! There's a part of you I've never reached, Lil. You always close the door!

LIL: *(Lightly.)* You and I were terrible together, Kitty. Just terrible. We competed with each other all the time. Our relationship was an exercise in "can you top this?"

KITTY: *(To* ANNIE.*)* She thought I was a coward when I stopped practicing medicine.

LIL: *(Lying, glances at* ANNIE.*)* No, I didn't.

ANNIE: *(Backing her up.)* She didn't.

KITTY: *(To both of them.)* I know.

LIL: Well, my mother always wanted me to marry a doctor.

ANNIE: And she thought you looked sexy in that white coat. I could never see it myself.

KITTY: Those two years with you, Lil, they were special.

LIL: Well, try to remember the good parts, will you?

KITTY: I don't ever want to forget beating on that door of that motel room. Every time I take myself seriously, I want to think of that. I must have looked like twelve kinds of a jackass.

LIL: You did. *(To* ANNIE.*)* She did. *(They laugh together.)*

KITTY: *(Through the laughter, to* ANNIE.*)* Don't let me forget that.

ANNIE: Count on it.

(The laughter awkwardly peters out. A moment of silence falls.)

LIL: *(Quietly.)* How much time do I have left, Kitty? *(KITTY can't answer. ANNIE turns away suddenly, about to cry. LIL puts her hand on ANNIE's shoulder. To ANNIE.)* Don't you go soft on me. I need you now.

ANNIE: *(Holding herself together.)* I'm here. I'm right here. *(LIL keeps her hand on ANNIE as though for support.)*

LIL: Answer me, Kitty.

KITTY: What are you asking me, Lil? How long on your feet and pain-free?

LIL: Yes. I have to know. I have to plan.

KITTY: Lil, there's new growth. It could accelerate—or you could go into remission again.

LIL: Is that likely?

KITTY: It happens sometimes.

LIL: The worst that could happen, Kitty. The bottom line.

KITTY: Don't put me in this position, Lil.

LIL: Six months?

ANNIE: Answer her, Kitty.

KITTY: Less.

LIL: Three?

KITTY: *(Hedging.)* Maybe.

LIL: Six weeks of feeling good?

KITTY: At least.

LIL: *(She'd expected more time—she is stunned.)* Why is this happening to me, Kitty? Why isn't it happening to you or Annie or Rita or Rae? Why not Donna, why not Sue? Are you all so much worthier than I am? I'm in love—for the first time in my life, I feel totally alive. Damn you! *(KITTY is helpless.)*

ANNIE: *(To KITTY.)* Do something. Help her. *(But KITTY can't.)*

LIL: *(Seeing KITTY's helplessness.)* It's all right.

ANNIE: *(Angry.)* It's not all right!

LIL: *(Comforting ANNIE.)* I'm going to fish with you, my friend, out on that rock—we're going to smoke the best stuff we can buy—and every day, the first one to catch two blues buys lunch and drinks at Molly Pitcher's.

ANNIE: *(Trying to be light.)* I'm not much good at fishing.

LIL: I'll teach you all my tricks. *(To KITTY.)* And you, you never beat me in a game of poker yet.

KITTY: *(Trying to be light.)* That's because you cheat.

LIL: Me? The Girl Scout? Cheat? Eight o'clock tonight—I'm going to teach you how to fake. Quarters.

KITTY: Aw, Lil. *Pennies.*

LIL: *Quarters*, Kitty. Tightwad. Geez. *(To* ANNIE.) I'm offering her trade secrets and she's hassling me over quarters. Now I ask you, is that gratitude?

(*During the above sequence,* RITA, RAE *and* EVA *enter.* EVA *is carrying a container of soup.)*

RAE: Don't slosh that. It's hot.

RITA: Her hands are shaking. *(She takes container from* EVA. *To* RAE.) Smells delicious.

(*Onstage,* LIL, ANNIE *and* KITTY *are continuing their moment of closeness. As this scene on the beach concludes, they move awkwardly apart on stage.)*

RAE: Actually, it's very bland. Kitty said to make something easy on her stomach. They've got her on a lot of medication. Don't let her load it with salt.

EVA: *(Uncomfortably close to the stairs.)* I wish someone had told me. . . . *(RAE touches* EVA *supportively.)*

RITA: Would it have made a difference?

EVA: I don't know. It might have. *(She takes bowl from* RITA *and steps onto the stairs, calls.)* Lil! *(The group onstage responds immediately.)*

ANNIE: *(To* LIL.*)* Hey, it's Eva.

KITTY: *(Admitting* EVA, RAE *and* RITA.*)* It took you that long to open a can of chicken noodle?

RAE: I made it from scratch! Only the best for Lil.

KITTY: She could have starved while we were waiting.

(EVA sees LIL—*they look at one another for a moment.)*

EVA: Soup. Rae made it for you. *(EVA puts it on counter.)*

LIL: Fuck Rae's soup. *(She opens her arms and* EVA *goes into them. They cling to one another.)*

RAE: *(In response to* LIL*'s line.)* Gee, thanks.

RITA: *(To* LIL.*)* Welcome home.

(RITA and RAE *attempt to welcome* LIL, *touching her shoulder, kissing her cheek, but she's oblivious to them, her attentions are all on* EVA.*)*

RAE: Ditto. *(But there is no response from* LIL.*)*

ANNIE: *(Having stuck her finger in the soup.)* This needs salt.

KITTY: She shouldn't have salt.

ANNIE: *(To RAE.)* It's too bland, honey, has no taste.

RAE: *(Observing LIL and EVA.)* Anybody get the feeling we're not wanted?

(The others agree and they start to move out. As they go:)

ANNIE: *(To LIL.)* Stay away from that soup, it's terrible.

KITTY: If you need me, Lil, I'll be on the beach.

RITA: *(Calls.)* She'll be in the cabin. *(To KITTY.)* You're going to bed. You've been at that hospital day and night.

KITTY: *(Stubbornly.)* I'll be on the beach, Lil.

RITA: *(Lovingly.)* Kitty, we haven't been alone together for a week. . . .

KITTY: *(Getting the picture.)* I'll be in the cabin, Lil.

ANNIE: *(As they exit, to RAE.)* Why don't we go to Molly Pitcher's and have lunch with Sue and Donna?

RAE: Because there's a pot of soup this big on the stove.

ANNIE: I was afraid of that.

(They are all offstage.)

LIL: *(Holding* EVA *apart and looking at her.)* Well, I'm back. Fit as a fiddle.

EVA: You're going to be just fine.

LIL: Oh, yeah, I always said I could lick this thing.

EVA: *(Uncomfortable.)* Don't let the soup get cold.

LIL: *(Aware of* EVA's *discomfort.)* You didn't know you were getting damaged merchandise, did you? I'm sorry, Eva.

EVA: Stop that.

LIL: It changes everything.

EVA: No, it doesn't. *(But it does.)* Soon as you get to feeling better, we'll go to Europe just like we planned.

LIL: Sure.

EVA: We'll go to Switzerland—we don't have to ski.

LIL: I couldn't tell you.

EVA: I know. *(Pause.)* We can still ride the chairlift up the Alps.

LIL: I just couldn't tell you.

EVA: Tiny villages sparkling in the snow. . . .

LIL: *(Sharply.)* There's no snow in Switzerland this time of year.

EVA: *(Forging ahead.)* We'll go to Amsterdam then. Maybe Rae and Annie will come with us. Somebody has to give me away.

LIL: Nobody can give you away, Eva. You don't belong to anybody but yourself.

EVA: You're upset. You're not feeling well.

LIL: I feel fine. Alley cats recover very quickly.

EVA: We'll travel for a while, then maybe rent a cottage in New England this fall—we can go to the movies and read books together—I can read your favorite books to you—

LIL: Do yourself a favor, Eva. Leave me.

EVA: You don't mean that.

LIL: I do. I bet I've had a hundred women in my life—what makes you think I'd want to spend the rest of my life with you? And your memories of George and your goddam furniture and your uptight mother?

EVA: Lil, don't.

LIL: I want to do some living before I die. *(She goes to door.)* Hey, anybody down there? Where's Donna? I want to see Donna! *(She turns to EVA coldly.)* Get out of here, Eva. Get out of my life. *(EVA doesn't budge.)*

EVA: That's always worked for you, hasn't it? One act of

bravado and you're off the hook. *(LIL is stunned.)* You have to catch the biggest fish, take every card game, seduce all the women you encounter—as long as you're winning, Lil, you're just fine. But when things get difficult, you leap out the motel window. We love each other, Lil. That's a commitment.

LIL: *(Quietly.)* Next summer, someone else will be standing at this window watching a July sunset—and Rae and Annie will be sitting over there, sipping drinks, and they'll say to this stranger at the window—"Beautiful sunset, huh? Lil loved that view. She thought God put that rock down there for her. When she stood on it with the surf pounding against it, spraying salt so high that she could taste it on her lips, she was Queen of Bluefish Cove." —I can't say goodbye to that beach out there, Eva. I can't say goodbye to Annie or to Kitty. How can I say goodbye to you? *(LIL goes to EVA, lets EVA hold her. EVA is now the strong one.)*

(As the lights dim to black, we hear KITTY and RITA's voices.)

RITA: The wind's so strong. I had no idea it got so cold along the beach.

KITTY: Well, we've never had the occasion to be out here in late fall.

RITA: Pull that scarf around your neck, darling, I don't want you to catch cold. You start the promotion tour for your new book next week and it would be disastrous if you developed laryngitis.

KITTY: What would you think if I were to open up my office again. . . .

RITA: You mean go back to practicing?

KITTY: Lil always felt that I was copping out.

(The lights are now up on the cabin and the beach. KITTY and RITA, dressed for winter, walk to the stairs; RAE, also dressed for winter, sits on the stairs. ANNIE stands on the rock, looking out to sea. RITA and KITTY mount the stairs.)

RAE: *(Glancing at her watch.)* I guess it's over now in Michigan. The service was at one o'clock.

RITA: I don't understand how they could take her. She wanted to be buried here.

KITTY: They're her family, honey. They have the legal right.

RITA: Her mother and father had disowned her.

KITTY: Well, they did fly here and stay by her at the end.

RITA: Stay by her? They guarded her from us.

(At the top of the stairs, they enter the cabin and begin to stack boxes and fold clothing for packing. EVA enters from the bathroom, carrying a box.)

SUE: I don't know what to do with all this stuff. Toothpaste, aspirin, bubblebath—

EVA: I promised Marge Eaton we'd clear this place out. Just put it over there, Sue.

KITTY: Lil asked me to give these clothes to the women's center. Some of them are pretty raggedy.

RITA: You can't give that workshirt to anybody. It's torn in half a dozen places.

KITTY: Well, throw it away then.

EVA: No. *(She takes it.)* I'd like to have that.

RITA: We could store these toiletries in our cabin for the winter —it's a shame to throw it all away.

SUE: What about this tackle box?

EVA: She wanted Annie to have that.

RITA: I'll take it down to her. *(She goes downstairs.)*

EVA: I wonder who'll have this place next summer?

KITTY: How about you, Eva?

EVA: I don't think so, Kitty. I couldn't afford it, anyway.

KITTY: You can always visit us.

EVA: I hope I'll be working next summer. I finish that office management course in January, thanks to Sue.

KITTY: If I open my practice again, I'll need an office manager.

EVA: *(Gratefully.)* Thanks. I've filled out applications for several big corporations with offices in Europe. I'd really like to travel. *(Smiles.)* Have some adventures.

KITTY: She loved you very much.

EVA: *(Pulling herself together.)* I know.

KITTY: *(Changing the subject.)* I expected to see Donna here today.

SUE: I don't think she knows, Kitty. I don't know where to contact her.

KITTY: That was the healthiest thing you ever did, Sue.

SUE: If you say so.

EVA: *(Looking around.)* Well, I think that's it. We can start carrying it down.

SUE: *(Calls.)* Hey, Rae, Rita, let's go.

(RAE *and* RITA *come upstairs and take bundles from* KITTY. *One by one, they begin to come down the stairs, arms loaded.* ANNIE *is squatting by* LIL's *tackle box, picking out the lures. As others come down the stairs, she leaps to the rock, holding one lure in her hand.)*

RAE: What is that, honey?

ANNIE: It's her favorite lure. She always used it for the blue-fish. *(Puts lure in tackle box.)* Next year, we're going to build a barbeque pit down here. It'll be our summer project.

RAE: My summer project is going to be to lie in the sun with my feet up.

KITTY: I don't know how much time I'll be able to spend out here next year—if I open up my practice, I'll have office hours weekdays—

RITA: I think I'll hate it when you're on call, you'll be tired all the time.

SUE: I wouldn't miss a summer at Bluefish Cove for anything—it somehow puts my whole year in perspective.

(They are off now except ANNIE and RAE. They look up at EVA in cabin.)

RAE: You coming, Eva?

EVA: *(Lowering blinds.)* Yes, I'm coming.

ANNIE: You need a hand?

EVA: No thanks, Annie. I can make it by myself.

(She lowers the blind between herself and audience. RAE and ANNIE exit, knowing EVA will soon follow.)

BLACKOUT

What the critics said....about Jane Chambers'

A LATE SNOW

"An important breakthrough...moving and convincing."
LOS ANGELES TIMES

"A well-crafted play with three-dimensional characters, rich humor, a believable story line and important statements"
THE CONNECTION

"Combines humor, decency and honesty with intelligent observations about the nature of human relationships...very, very funny." **NEW YORK THEATRE VOICE**

"An important play that should be seen by everyone, straight, gay or on the fringe."
DRAMA-LOGUE

"One warm, wonderful play"
NEW YORK NATIVE

A LATE SNOW

A PLAY IN TWO ACTS BY

Jane Chambers

reprinted from the
JH PRESS
GAY PRESS SCRIPT SERIES
by

T 'n' T CLASSICS, INC.

BOOKS

are explosive

360 WEST 36 ST. #2NW
NEW YORK NY 10018-6412
212-736-6279: FAX - 212-695-3219

A LATE SNOW was produced at the Clark Center for the Performing Arts, in 1974. Produced by Playwrights Horizons; directed by Nyla Lyon; costumes by Sally Blankfield; lighting design by Patrika Brown. In the original cast:

QUINCEY .. Carolyn Cope (replaced by Lin Shaye)
PAT .... Susan Sullivan
ELLIE .... Susanne Wasson
MARGO .... Anita Keal
PEGGY .... Marilyn Hamlin

A LATE SNOW was revived by Meridian Gay Theatre, Terry Helbing and Terry Miller, producers, at the Urban Arts Theatre, opening September 15, 1983. Directed by Francine L. Trevens; scenic design by Leon Munier; lighting design by Peter Anderson; costume/prop coordination by Lynn Marrapodi; assistant director: Jeannine Haas; stage manager: Janine Trevens.

QUINCEY .... Kathryn Shield
PAT .... Jere Jacob
ELLIE .... Maggie Suter
MARGO .... Pamela H. Osowski
PEGGY .... Hollace Colburn

In order of appearance:
QUINCEY: Mid-twenties, pleasant, open, honest, a young writer.
PAT: Mid-thirties, tall, attractive, witty. A charming alcoholic.
ELLIE: Mid-thirties, attractive, cool. A college professor.
MARGO: Forties, a well-known writer, attractive, self-contained, super-charming.
PEGGY: Mid-thirties, a chic suburban housewife trying to do everything "right."

ACT ONE

It is late afternoon in early spring. As the curtain rises, we see the interior of a cabin by a lake.

Downstairs, a living room and a kitchen, somehow separated from one another. The living room has a fireplace, although we need not see the fire. It also has a big window overlooking the lake, which can be the "fourth wall."

The second floor, which can be indicated by risers, has two small bedrooms and a door leading to a bath. There should be steps of some kind from one level to the other, indicating a stairway.

Downstairs, there are two doors: a front door, off the living room; a back door, off the kitchen.

Furnishings are comfortable and worn. Books and artifacts are tossed comfortably around. There is a bar area in the living room and a set of wind chimes in the master bedroom window.

QUINCEY opens the door to the living room from the outside with a key.

QUINCEY: I hope you can get that truck back out of here.

PAT'S VOICE: Oh, sure. It's got four-wheel drive. Just prop the door open.

(QUINCEY *does so.*)

PAT'S VOICE: I've got the tailgate down. We can roll it in. Come on.

(QUINCEY *goes back out. We hear the sound of something heavy being moved.*)

QUINCEY'S VOICE: It weighs a ton.

PAT'S VOICE: You wouldn't listen. I tried to sell you something nice and light—an end table, a dry sink. . . .

QUINCEY'S VOICE: This is the piece she wants. She talks about it all the time.

(*They appear, pushing an antique Dutch cupboard.*)

PAT'S VOICE: Lift it over the sill.

QUINCEY: (*Looking at the heavy object*) Lift it over the sill.

PAT: Come on.

(*With a mighty effort,* QUINCEY *does so.*)

QUINCEY: Mother of God.

PAT: Good. Now we just roll it into place.

QUINCEY: It goes over there.

PAT: I know where it goes.

QUINCEY: Watch the rug.

PAT: Push!

QUINCEY: Don't scratch it!

PAT: Just push, will you?

QUINCEY: Don't scrape the floor!

PAT: You're really uptight, aren't you? (*She pushes the piece into place, scraping the floor.*)

QUINCEY: You scraped the floor! (*She looks closely.*) Shit.

PAT: Spit on it. (QUINCEY *looks at her, puzzled.*) Spit on it and rub it with your finger.

QUINCEY: (*Does so.*) It's a gouge.

PAT: It's a scratch. She'll never notice. You can't hurt these floors. (QUINCEY *continues to spit and rub.*) What does she do, beat you?

QUINCEY: I'm not even supposed to be out here. I mean, she's never said, "Here are the keys, go out to the cabin."

PAT: Aren't you here every weekend?

QUINCEY: With Ellie. After all, it's her house.

PAT: It's her house. (*She looks around.*) It looks the same. I miss it. (*Quickly*) I never did like that piece. It's junk.

QUINCEY: Why did you take it?

PAT: Because Ellie wanted it. I figured some sucker would buy it.

QUINCEY: Ellie says you took half the stuff in the place.

PAT: Well, half of it was mine. She took the lamp. I wanted that. (*She indicates a Tiffany shade.*) That's worth something—a couple of hundred.

QUINCEY: Don't touch that!

PAT: Just looking.

QUINCEY: (*About scratch*) I hope she won't notice.

PAT: She will.

QUINCEY: You said she wouldn't!

PAT: (*Smiles*) I lied. (*She examines shade closely.*) If I put this in the shop tomorrow morning, it'd be sold by noon. Three hundred, easy.

QUINCEY: Come on, don't touch that!

PAT: Red glass is rare. Do you know why?

QUINCEY: Leave it alone!

PAT: They use gold to make red glass. Gold.

QUINCEY: Please. I never should have brought you out here.

PAT: You wanted delivery. You drove a hard bargain.

QUINCEY: Bullshit. I paid you twice what that piece is worth.

PAT: That's true. Actually, you paid much more than twice. Ellie and I found that piece of junk in an abandoned barn, four years ago.

QUINCEY: (*Defensively*) She loves it. She's always saying, "I wish I had my old cupboard." She kept her papers in it, I think.

PAT: Her private treasure chest. I used to love to go through it when she was out of the house. She kept little notebooks. . . .

QUINCEY: She still does. She has an old library table in the apartment. She keeps her notebooks in the drawer.

PAT: "Pat drunk seventeen days this month. Rash on my right hand getting worse. Psychological? Order a cord of wood by the thirtieth." A veritable font of information, huh?

QUINCEY: I don't know. I never look.

PAT: You should. Ellie rarely tells you what she's really thinking. "Pat's stories too pat. Something's going on."

QUINCEY: I shouldn't have brought you out here.

PAT: I still have keys.

QUINCEY: She changed the lock.

PAT: She take a Peace Bond out on me, too?

QUINCEY: Ellie says you'd steal the gold from your grandmother's teeth.

PAT: (*Grins.*) There's a lot of stuff here I'd like to have.

QUINCEY: It belongs to Ellie.

PAT: It belongs to both of us.

QUINCEY: Not any more.

PAT: Where'd you get those keys?

QUINCEY: I took them out of her bureau drawer.

PAT: Before you establish your territorial prerogative, you'd better get your own keys. (*She goes to bar.*) Want a drink?

QUINCEY: We can't stay.

PAT: Why'd you come to my shop?

QUINCEY: To buy that cupboard.

PAT: Really?

QUINCEY: It's our anniversary. Our first anniversary. I want to give her something special.

PAT: When is it?—your anniversary? What's the date?

QUINCEY: The eighteenth.

PAT: Amazing. Sure you won't join me? (*She continues to case the house as she drinks.*)

QUINCEY: We've got to go.

PAT: No hurry. I've closed shop for the day.

QUINCEY: We shouldn't stay out here.

PAT: The eighteenth of April. Ours was June twenty-fourth. It wasn't really, but I convinced Ellie it was—it was close enough. All my anniversaries are June twenty-fourth. It's the only way I can remember: 6-24—the first three digits of my social security. (*She picks up an object.*)

QUINCEY: Come on. Don't.

PAT: Why'd you come to my shop?

QUINCEY: (*Taking object from her*) It was the only way to get the cupboard.

PAT: There are a couple of cupboards just like that every weekend at the flea market.

QUINCEY: That cupboard is special.

PAT: It looks like all the others. She wouldn't know the difference. . . . You've walked by before. I've seen you.

QUINCEY: You lived with her for five years. You were an important part of her life.

PAT: (*Satisfied*) I never should have let her buy me out.

QUINCEY: You made her buy you out!

PAT: She wouldn't let me live here and I needed the money.

QUINCEY: She didn't have it.

PAT: She got it though. She could always get money if she had to. The pleasures of a Good Credit rating. (*Pause*) We laid these floors ourselves—and framed the windows—

QUINCEY: We've got to go now.

PAT: Ellie's mother sent us those drapes.

QUINCEY: It'll be dark soon.

PAT: So what? You said she won't be back until Sunday.

QUINCEY: The conference isn't over until Saturday night. She's flying back on Sunday.

PAT: When we bought this place there was no insulation, no paneling, you could see the ground through the floorboards.

QUINCEY: Please, Pat, let's go.

PAT: She's really got you tied up, hasn't she? Little Miss Step and Fetch It. Ellie loves to give orders. I never took them. (*She goes back to bar.*) Are you a teetotaler, too?

QUINCEY: No. Are you going to be able to drive?

PAT: My reputation precedes me.

QUINCEY: Ellie says you have a problem.

PAT: (*Pours them each a drink.*) Ellie says I'm a drunk. She's at a conference?

QUINCEY: In Philadelphia. University department heads.

PAT: She go alone?

QUINCEY: With the other university department heads.

PAT: I never knew a conference to end on a Saturday night. (*She hands* QUINCEY *a drink.*) Cheers. (*At window*) When did the ice go this year?

QUINCEY: Sometime last week, I think.

PAT: We used to bet on the day.

QUINCEY: We weren't out here.

PAT: Ever see it go?

QUINCEY: No.

PAT: It starts melting around the edges. For a few days, it's slush for maybe fifteen, twenty feet around the shoreline. Then the circle of ice that's left in the middle of the lake gets gray, then black—then WHOOSH. It goes under in ten seconds. The black lake turns navy, then sky blue. And it's spring. (*She surveys the cabin.*) You a student of Ellie's?

QUINCEY: I was—last year when I was in grad school. I'm a writer.

PAT: Published?

QUINCEY: No.

PAT: How do you earn a living?

QUINCEY: I edit a throwaway.

PAT: What?

QUINCEY: One of those four-page weekly papers with neighborhood news and a lot of ads that you find in your mailbox.

PAT: I didn't know Ellie was into seducing her students.

QUINCEY: She's not. I pursued her. It wasn't easy. She wasn't over you.

PAT: Oh?

QUINCEY: I lived with your ghost for months.

PAT: She never answered my letters. She hung up when I called her.

QUINCEY: Five years is a long time.

PAT: Yes, it is.

QUINCEY: It takes a while to get over it. She's over it now.

PAT: Chilly in here. Let's start a fire.

QUINCEY: Let's go.

PAT: There's wood in the crib by the fireplace. You know how to start a fire?

QUINCEY: Of course.

PAT: Well, do it. I'm going to take a look upstairs.

QUINCEY: No.

PAT: (*Charming*) She'll never know.

QUINCEY: No.

PAT: For old times' sake.

QUINCEY: No.

PAT: (*Handing her the starter wood*) Placate me. Lonely, nearing middle age, with a slight tendency to imbibe, a pitiful figure . . . (QUINCEY *laughs in spite of herself.*) Good girl.

QUINCEY: Don't take anything!

PAT: (*Going upstairs*) You can frisk me when I come down.

(QUINCEY *begins to make a fire. We hear a car motor, see lights flash across the kitchen.* QUINCEY *looks up quizzically as the key turns in the back door.*

ELLIE *enters.*)

QUINCEY: Oh, shit.

ELLIE: Quincey!

QUINCEY: You're back early!

(QUINCEY *embraces* ELLIE, *who responds perfunctorily, then pulls nervously away.* ELLIE *is dismayed by* QUINCEY's *unexpected presence but tries valiantly not to show it.*)

QUINCEY: I wanted to surprise you!

ELLIE: You did.

(QUINCEY *pulls* ELLIE *to the cupboard.*)

QUINCEY: With this. (*She hugs* ELLIE.) Happy First Anniversary!

ELLIE: Quincey, where did you get this?

(*At the back door,* MARGO *appears, suitcase in hand. She stands there, unnoticed.*)

QUINCEY: (*About the cupboard*) Surprise!

ELLIE: Where did you get it?

QUINCEY: It's what you wanted!

ELLIE: It's just like the old one.

QUINCEY: It *is* the old one.

MARGO: May I come in?

(ELLIE *looks from* MARGO *to* QUINCEY, *back to* MARGO. *She is flustered.*)

QUINCEY: Hello.

MARGO: Hello.

ELLIE: (*Recovering*) This is Quincey Evans, a former student of mine. Quincey, Margo Bettis.

QUINCEY: Margo. *The* Margo Bettis?

MARGO: The only one I know.

QUINCEY: *A Memory of Autumn, The Last Question, Miller's Breach, Afternoon in . . .*

MARGO: Amazing.

QUINCEY: I took a course in you. Ellie teaches a course in you.

MARGO: I know. Margot Bettis a multiple-choice answer.

QUINCEY: You're always an essay. I thought you were retired (*Catches herself.*)—a recluse. I thought you never came out in public.

MARGO: Only after dark.

QUINCEY: I mean, you never give interviews, or . . . (*Shrugs.*) I'm getting in deeper, aren't I? Sorry. Welcome. (*To* ELLIE) Where did you find her?

ELLIE: Margo was the guest lecturer at the conference. We flew back together.

MARGO: She's trying to coerce me into teaching.

ELLIE: A lecture series. Wouldn't that be a coup?

QUINCEY: Terrific. You're a kind of cult among the undergrads.

MARGO: It terrifies me.

QUINCEY: I have everything you've ever written.

ELLIE: I asked Margo to spend the day here tomorrow—so I can do my sales pitch.

QUINCEY: It's like seeing a legend come to life.

ELLIE: I promised her a quiet day by the lake.

QUINCEY: I hope we'll have time to talk. I have a thousand questions.

ELLIE: I have yet to sell her on the joys of university life.

QUINCEY: I'm a writer, too, you know. Fledgling but good, I think.

MARGO: Ellie, I'm tired . . . and a little uncomfortable. Can I change?

ELLIE: Of course. Upstairs. Excuse us, Quincey.

(ELLIE *picks up* MARGO's *bag, starts up the stairs. She encounters* PAT *on her way down.* ELLIE *is startled and angry at* PAT's *presence.*)

PAT: Hi.

ELLIE: What are you doing here?

PAT: I came with the cupboard.

QUINCEY: She insisted: free delivery.

PAT: (*To* ELLIE) Thank you?

ELLIE: Thank you. Excuse us, please.

(*She leads* MARGO, *bewildered, upstairs.* MARGO *stops at the master bedroom.*

MARGO: What a cozy room. And a beautiful view of the lake.

ELLIE: Yes. (*Pause.*) Put your things anywhere.

MARGO: But this is your room, isn't it?

ELLIE: It's the nicest room. The guest room is kind of sparse. I'll sleep there.

MARGO: No.

ELLIE: Please. I insist.

MARGO: No. It's your room.

ELLIE: The guest room overlooks the compost heap. Please?

MARGO: All right.

ELLIE: It's the least I can do. (*Pause.*) I'm sorry. I didn't expect anyone to be here.

MARGO: (*Smiles.*) It's a regular party, isn't it?

ELLIE: They'll be leaving soon.

MARGO: It's all right.

ELLIE: It's not all right. I promised you a quiet weekend.

MARGO: They're your friends. I'm sure they're interesting people. (*She starts to undress.*) Aren't they?

ELLIE: (*Ignoring that*) I know how you feel about meeting strangers.

MARGO: That's my problem. I'm a big girl now. I can take care of myself.

ELLIE: I'm sorry about Quincey. She's young and exuberant. She didn't mean to embarrass you.

MARGO: Embarrass me? I was flattered. Would you hand me that shirt, please?

(*Downstairs.*)

PAT: (*To* QUINCEY) Well, well. Aren't you glad we stuck around?

QUINCEY: Cool it. That's business.

PAT: I'll say.

QUINCEY: Don't you know who she is?

PAT: I heard your eulogy.

QUINCEY: She's like a myth. I've never seen a picture of her. I've read everything she's ever written, but I never knew what she looked like before.

PAT: You won't forget.

QUINCEY: Ellie has many business associates. That's what this is. I know Ellie.

PAT: I guess I don't. I thought she was true-blue-lou.

QUINCEY: She is.

(*Upstairs,* ELLIE *is uncomfortable watching* MARGO.)

ELLIE: They won't stay long.

MARGO: Will you stop worrying?

ELLIE: Sorry. I'll go downstairs and take care of it. (*Pause.*) Are you all right?

MARGO: I'm fine. Just fine.

(ELLIE *descends the stairs as* PAT *is pouring another drink.*)

ELLIE: Quincey? Thank you. (*She hugs* QUINCEY *warmly.*) I'm sorry I was abrupt—I was just stunned to find you here.

QUINCEY: It's all right.

ELLIE: It was an opportunity that I couldn't pass up, honey. Every university in the country has tried to get Margo on faculty. No one's ever succeeded. We seemed to hit it off at the conference. . . . Honey, she doesn't know. . . . I mean, I haven't said anything. So, play it cool?

QUINCEY: I hate doing that.

ELLIE: Please?

QUINCEY: It's important to you, isn't it?

PAT: (*Entering their area*) So, how are you, Ellie?

ELLIE: Fine, Pat. And you?

PAT: Fine.

ELLIE: Good.

PAT: You look well.

ELLIE: So do you.

PAT: The house looks good.

ELLIE: It's a nice house.

PAT: It always was, I miss it.

ELLIE: It's been good seeing you, Pat. I appreciate your bringing the cupboard out. You don't mind giving Quincey a ride back to town, do you?

PAT: (*Pause.*) I see.

ELLIE: I have work to do.

QUINCEY: I'd like to stay, Ellie. I'd like to talk to her.

ELLIE: If I get her to sign a contract, you'll have lots of chances to talk to her. (*Pause.*) It wouldn't look good, honey. I'm sorry, Quincey.

(PAT *grins.* MARGO *comes down the stairs, sloppy, comfortable.*)

MARGO: This is the real person. That other lady is a sham.

PAT: Hi.

ELLIE: Oh. Margo, this is Pat Leonard.

PAT: I've read your work.

MARGO: And?

PAT: You're good.

QUINCEY: Great.

MARGO: You really are a fan, aren't you?

QUINCEY: An admirer. Fan sounds—childish.

PAT: You must be used to adulation.

MARGO: Not at all. I don't see many people. That's one of the things that distresses me about Ellie's idea.

QUINCEY: Lecturing.

MARGO: It terrifies me. All those people!

QUINCEY: Adoring you.

MARGO: Why? For what?

QUINCEY: For being one of the best writers in the world.

MARGO: She's tenacious.

PAT: Ellie can testify to that.

ELLIE: I don't know what you're talking about.

PAT: Quincey told me about your first meeting.

MARGO: Oh? (*Pause.*) Well?

QUINCEY: It's not a very interesting story. I want to talk to you. If I could have picked any writer in the world to interview, it would have been you: and here you are.

MARGO: I'm overwhelmed. I'm also hungry. How about some supper?

ELLIE: Pat and Quincey have to get back to town.

MARGO: We bought plenty of food—Ellie and I stopped in this marvelous little country store. . . .

PAT: O'Brien's.

MARGO: You know it?

PAT: Well.

MARGO: And I'm cooking.

ELLIE: No.

MARGO: Yes. Does that tempt you?

QUINCEY: Ellie . . .

PAT: We'd love to stay.

MARGO: Good!

QUINCEY: We'll leave right after supper.

MARGO: You (*To* ELLIE) go upstairs and change. Get comfortable. You two (*To* PAT *and* QUINCEY) bring in the groceries. (ELLIE, *reluctantly, starts for stairs.*) Go on! (PAT *grins and goes for the groceries.* QUINCEY *tries to elicit some response from* ELLIE, *but* ELLIE *goes upstairs. To* QUINCEY) I neglected to mention that I haven't cooked since Thanksgiving three years ago when my sister was having her fifth baby.

QUINCEY: How do you eat?

MARGO: I live in a hotel. There's a restaurant downstairs.

QUINCEY: That must be expensive.

MARGO: Money buys time. And time is something a writer never has enough of. You'll find that out.

QUINCEY: You live alone?

MARGO: Yes.

QUINCEY: I don't think I'll ever want to live alone.

MARGO: You never have?

QUINCEY: No. My family, then college, then—roommates.

MARGO: You should try it alone. Everyone should. Builds an independent person.

QUINCEY: I always want to have a lover.

MARGO: Just don't get married and have babies. It drains your creative juices.

QUINCEY: That isn't exactly what I had in mind.

MARGO: You have a boyfriend?

QUINCEY: Well, I have had a boyfriend. A lot of them, as a matter of fact.

MARGO: I should think so. You're a nice-looking girl.

(PAT *enters with groceries.*)

PAT: You're not doing your share, Quincey, friend.

QUINCEY: Oh. Sorry. I'll get the rest.

PAT: That's it.

MARGO: Don't stand there like Samson. Those must be heavy. Put them down. (PAT *does.*) I hope there's no one here with a weight problem. (*She takes spaghetti out of the bag.*) We're having spaghetti. Fan—admirer—want to help?

QUINCEY: Sure.

PAT: You never got that fire going, did you?

(*Without waiting for an answer,* PAT *heads to the fireplace.*

ELLIE *comes down the stairs.*)

ELLIE: (*To kitchen*) Everything under control?

MARGO: Fine. The fan—

QUINCEY: Admirer.

MARGO: —is helping.

ELLIE: What can I do?

MARGO: Nothing. Out of the kitchen! Too many cooks . . .

ELLIE: You're sure? If you need me . . .

(*As* ELLIE *enters living room:*)

PAT: I need you. Give me some newspapers off that pile.

ELLIE: (*Doing so*) You always had a talent for that.

PAT: You haven't had a fire since.

ELLIE: Don't flatter yourself. I've managed.

PAT: You still think I'm a scoundrel, don't you?

ELLIE: Aren't you?

PAT: I never thought so.

ELLIE: Pat, I don't want to get into that.

PAT: I didn't mean to be.

ELLIE: It's over, let's forget it. Okay?

PAT: It's not over. The ice sank last week.

ELLIE: I didn't see it.

PAT: It's going to be spring.

ELLIE: It looks like snow to me.

PAT: All dead things come to life.

ELLIE: No. It looks like snow.

PAT: I'm sorry. You never gave me a chance to say I'm sorry. You wouldn't see me, talk to me. You never gave us a chance.

ELLIE: (*Pause.*) Did you give Cassie a chance?

PAT: I never loved her.

ELLIE: You made love to her—drunk. You wrapped her in a car around a walnut tree and you walked away.

PAT: It was an accident.

ELLIE: She was my friend.

PAT: You hated her.

ELLIE: I hated her for having for affair with you, for making a fool out of me, for lying to me. For loving you.

PAT: It didn't mean anything, Ellie. It never meant anything.

ELLIE: Cassie's dead, Pat. That means something.

PAT: It was an accident.

ELLIE: Everything's an accident. It's an accident you drink too much. It's an accident you fall into bed with the nearest available woman. It's an accident that they all fall in love with you, even when you don't want them. Cassie is dead and you say, it was an accident.

PAT: Don't you think I feel anything?

ELLIE: I don't know.

PAT: I didn't want to kill anybody. I never wanted to hurt anybody. I'm sorry Cassie's dead. I'm sorry, sorry, sorry, I've said it a million times, asleep and awake. I know there's no price on a human life but I've paid, Ellie, I've paid. The court wiped out my trust fund; my father, the compassionate bastard, wiped me out of his will. I lost my home, I nearly lost my business. And I lost you.

ELLIE: I was just someone to come home to between binges, between affairs. Not much of a loss, Pat.

PAT: I loved you.

ELLIE: (*Pause.*) I loved you.

PAT: What happened to us?

ELLIE: Maybe five years is too long.

PAT: I wanted to be with you for a lifetime. I had a dream: two crochety old ladies rocking on that front porch, waiting for the ice to go. (*Pause.*) She's not enough for you, Ellie. You need more than that.

ELLIE: She's bright and honest—and she loves me.

PAT: She's there when you come home. Faithful and comfortable. Only a year and you're bored to death.

ELLIE: That's not true.

PAT: Then why the house guest?

ELLIE: The house guest is here on business. I don't know anything about her—personal preferences.

PAT: But you've got a feeling, haven't you?

(QUINCEY *enters the living room.*)

QUINCEY: Ellie, do we have a garlic press?

PAT: (*Smartly*) Bottom drawer on the left, under the sink.

QUINCEY: Ellie?

ELLIE: That's right.

(QUINCEY *exits.*)

PAT: Little Miss Step and Fetch It. But cute. I'll admit that. Cute.

ELLIE: You're jealous.

PAT: Not of her.

ELLIE: She's good for me.

PAT: She worships you. Good for your ego.

ELLIE: You won't give up ,will you?

PAT: She's no challenge. That's what makes the knees tremble and the wind chimes ring: the challenge. Without it, boredom.

ELLIE: If challenge means sitting up night after night wondering in whose bed you'll find your drunken lover, I've had enough challenge for a lifetime, thanks.

(*From the kitchen,* MARGO's *voice.*)

MARGO: All right, you two. I need some help!

PAT: (*To* ELLIE) Obviously, you haven't. (*To* MARGO) Coming!

(*They go into the kitchen.*)

MARGO: (*To* ELLIE) I understand you make magnificent sauce.

PAT: She does.

MARGO: (*To* PAT) And what are you good at?

PAT: (*Grinning*) My specialty is—mixing drinks.

ELLIE: (*Warning*) Pat . . .

MARGO: Mine is drinking them. (*To* ELLIE, *about the kitchen*) It's all yours. Let me know when you're ready for the spaghetti to go in.

(PAT *and* MARGO *go into the living room,* ELLIE *looking worriedly after them.*)

QUINCEY: (*To* ELLIE) Hi. I love you. I missed you.

(ELLIE *smiles nervously, proceeds to make sauce.* QUINCEY *presses garlic, cuts bread, etc.*

In the living room:)

MARGO: Straight up. A shot glass is fine.

PAT: I can tell you're my kind of woman.

(*In the kitchen:*)

QUINCEY: I'm jealous.

ELLIE: Don't be silly. I don't even know the woman.

QUINCEY: Not her. Pat.

ELLIE: I was crazy for five years. I won't go back.

QUINCEY: Sometimes I think you're still in love with her.

ELLIE: (*Ignoring that*) She's getting drunk, Quincey. You've got to get her out of here right after supper. Can you drive that truck of hers?

QUINCEY: I suppose so.

ELLIE: She's uncontrollable when she's drunk. She talks too much.

QUINCEY: That could be embarrassing.

ELLIE: And she'll try to seduce anyone—if she thinks it'll hurt me.

QUINCEY: Don't worry. I wouldn't fall for that.

(*In the living room:*)

MARGO: (*At window*) It looks like snow.

PAT: No way. It's too late in the season.

MARGO: It's a snow sky. (*She accepts drink.*) Thank you. So, exactly who are you?

PAT: (*Looking at sky*) A friend.

MARGO: Oh?

PAT: An ex-friend.

MARGO: You don't know which?

PAT: Like the weather up here, it could change any minute.

MARGO: You're from this area?

PAT: I lived here for five years. In this house.

MARGO: Oh. Ellie bought it from you?

PAT: Partly.

MARGO: What do you do?

PAT: I restore old things. Antiques.

MARGO: How about old writers?

PAT: I could open a department. (*Pause.*) You're not old.

MARGO: No? I had my success so early. I peaked at twenty-five—and there are too many years left after that. Girl Genius goes dry.

PAT: You're still writing.

MARGO: Trying. Strange. I had so much to say when I was twenty-five.

PAT: Does a writer write from imagination or experience?

MARGO: Experience first. That triggers the imagination.

PAT: And you're short on experience?

MARGO: (*Pause.*) Interesting.

PAT: Are you?

MARGO: Yes. Ten years ago I closed the door. I'd had as much experience as I could bear. Enough to last, I thought. (PAT *pours another drink, looks questioningly at* MARGO.) Not yet. But meeting Ellie this week . . .

PAT: Yes?

MARGO: So full of life, of ideas. I never thought of teaching.

PAT: Ellie loves it.

MARGO: It frightens me.

PAT: It's a challenge.

MARGO: Ellie makes me feel that I can do it. She makes me feel alive again—brave.

PAT: I see.

MARGO: (*Quickly, to kitchen*) How are you doing in there?

(*From kitchen:*)

ELLIE: Under way. (*To* QUINCEY) Go in the living room, honey. Relax.

QUINCEY: I'd rather stay with you.

ELLIE: I'd rather you kept an eye on Pat.

QUINCEY: (*Reluctantly*) Oh. (*She gives* ELLIE *a kiss as she goes into the living room.* ELLIE *gives her a warning look.*) Sorry. Just doing what comes naturally. (*She goes into the living room.*)

MARGO: Whatever it is, it smells good.

QUINCEY: It'll be good. Ellie's a super cook.

PAT: (*To* QUINCEY) You think everybody's just wonderful, don't you?

QUINCEY: (*To* PAT) Not necessarily.

MARGO: (*Quickly*) I'm sure Ellie cooks as well as she does everything else.

PAT: We're obviously all aware of Ellie's talents.

QUINCEY: (*Confused, quickly*) Tell me about the conference.

MARGO: The conference?

QUINCEY: In Philadelphia.

MARGO: Oh. Well, I gave a timid little lecture and Ellie led the applause.

QUINCEY: Where did you stay?

MARGO: The Concord.

QUINCEY: So did Ellie.

MARGO: Yes. Everyone at the conference stayed at the Concord. It's a lovely old hotel.

QUINCEY: I've never been there. I've never been to a conference.

PAT: You haven't missed a thing.

MARGO: You meet, have assemblies, lectures. . . .

QUINCEY: Day and night?

MARGO: Days mostly. There was a terrible dinner the first night—a command performance. Shoeleather steaks, frozen vegetables and speakers. Deadly. Everyone glued themselves to the bar afterward, I'm told. The turnout at the early session the next morning must have been very small.

QUINCEY: Ellie doesn't drink.

MARGO: We didn't stay. We spent the evening talking.

QUINCEY: In your room?

MARGO: In hers. (*To* PAT) Would you freshen this?

QUINCEY: Me, too.

PAT: (*To* QUINCEY) Oh. Sorry. (*She starts to mix drink.*) We need ice. I'll get it. (*She goes to kitchen.*)

ELLIE: (*To* PAT) Will you take it easy?

PAT: Nag, nag. I'm just being the genial host.

ELLIE: —ess.

PAT: (*Prissy*) Hostess.

ELLIE: The trouble with you is you don't like women.

PAT: Are you kidding?

ELLIE: You don't. Not really. You don't like yourself and you don't like other women.

PAT: Stop philosophizing and keep cooking. (*She slaps* ELLIE *on the ass and exits to living room with ice.*)

MARGO: I know that I'd enjoy working with Ellie.

PAT: (*Entering*) Ice, coming up.

(*In the kitchen,* ELLIE *tosses her apron on the sink and heads to the living room.*)

MARGO: But I'm nervous about making a commitment—to teaching.

ELLIE: (*Entering*) The sauce is simmering. You can put on the water for the spaghetti.

MARGO: (*Charmingly to* QUINCEY) Would you?

ELLIE: (*Before* QUINCEY *can answer*) Thanks, honey.

(QUINCEY, *irritated, goes to kitchen.*)

PAT: We were having a fascinating conversation: how you and Margo discovered one another across a crowded room in Philadelphia.

MARGO: That's not quite what I said.

PAT: And changed the course of one another's lives.

ELLIE: Pat!

MARGO: Of my life. I said that meeting you was meaningful to me. (*An awkward pause.*) And it might well change the course of my life. (*Laughs.*) It's a course that could use some changing, believe me.

PAT: (*To* ELLIE) Your boundless enthusiasm and zest for challenge has sparked new life, presented new horizons.

ELLIE: I've always admired Margo's work.

PAT: Presto! A marriage—of talents.

ELLIE: Will you shut up?

(MARGO *and* ELLIE *smile at each other.*)

PAT: (*In frustration*) Where's the poker. I want to stoke the fire.

ELLIE: (*Crossing to the window*) I don't know. In the crib. Look for it.

MARGO: Pat used to live here, she was telling me.

ELLIE: She was?

PAT: We used to live here together.

MARGO: I thought perhaps something like that. (ELLIE *looks at her quickly.*) You're snippy with each other. You must know each other very well.

PAT: Perceptive.

MARGO: It goes with being a writer. Occupational handicap—or advantage. Depends on your point of view.

PAT: She lives with Quincey now.

   (ELLIE *looks sharply at* PAT.)

MARGO: Oh.

ELLIE: (*Quickly*) We share an apartment near the university. Rents are very high.

MARGO: And you. Do you have a roommate, Pat?

PAT: Sometimes. And sometimes not.

MARGO: I guess I'm the only loner here. I have had rcommates though. (ELLIE *and* PAT *look with interest.*) I remember my college roommate. (*She laughs.*)

PAT: I never had a college roommate. Ellie did.

MARGO: Mine had peroxide hair. Frizzy. She lost her virginity in the entrance hall, after hours, her freshman year. Bled all over the bathroom. Put me in a state of terror: I was sure that going to bed with a man was tantamount to a seige of battle.

PAT: Wasn't it?

(MARGO *just smiles.*)

ELLIE: My college roommate was beautiful. The most beautiful girl on campus. The jocks used to line up in the lounge, waiting for her. She gave them all a hard time.

PAT: Perfect Peggy. (*To* MARGO) You'll excuse my attitude but I've heard this story a thousand times.

MARGO: You're about to hear it again. I'm interested.

ELLIE: No. (*Pause.*) She was just perfect, that's all.

MARGO: (*Easily*) And you loved her.

ELLIE: (*Taken aback*) Yes.

MARGO: It's nice to remember friends we've loved. What happened to her?

PAT: Perfect Peggy panicked. She got married.

MARGO: That's nice. Do you hear from her?

ELLIE: Christmas cards, now and then.

MARGO: You should look her up. It's fun to see how people change.

ELLIE: I'd rather remember her.

PAT: You can control your memories. You don't have to remember that she had a large wart on the back of her ear. . . .

ELLIE: She didn't have any warts!

PAT: Or she picked her nose.

ELLIE: Pat!

PAT: Or she drank a little too much. (*She pours herself another drink.*)

ELLIE: Stop it.

PAT: Or she fooled around. . . . (*She offers* MARGO *a drink.* MARGO *refuses.*) You can shine memories up real nice. But live people—they're a little harder to control.

ELLIE: (*Quickly*) I wrote to her recently, as a matter of fact. I told her about the cabin and invited her to bring her family up some weekend.

PAT: No kidding?

ELLIE: I don't know why I did that. I was—

PAT: Bored. (ELLIE *looks sharply at* PAT.) I'd like to meet Perfect Peggy.

ELLIE: I hope that can be avoided. (QUINCEY *enters, pours another drink.*) How's it going, Quincey? (QUINCEY *doesn't respond.*) Take it easy. You're not a drinker. (QUINCEY *slugs it.*) Are you all right?

QUINCEY: I think I'm not going to feel so good.

ELLIE: Go upstairs and lie down.

QUINCEY: Not on your life.

MARGO: We were talking about college roommates. Did you have a college roommate, Quincey?

PAT: Yeah. The professor.

QUINCEY: I only lived in the dorm six months. It wasn't my style. I couldn't feel free there. It's an up-tight school. (*To* ELLIE) Sorry, it's true.

MARGO: What do you mean, "up-tight"?

PAT: It means closed up tight, constipated.

ELLIE: Pat!

MARGO: I know what the word means. I haven't been dead—just cloistered.

QUINCEY: For instance: (*A pause. She doesn't know whether to go ahead or not.*) One person, a sophomore, tried to form a Gay Lib group. . . .

MARGO: Gay Lib? (*To* PAT) I know what it means.

PAT: I figured you did.

MARGO: (*To* QUINCEY) And?

QUINCEY: They kicked her out of the dorm.

MARGO: Who did?

QUINCEY: The administration. The rest of the kids, we rallied and picketed and the trustees had a hearing. They let her stay in school—

if she lived off campus. She couldn't live in the dorm.

ELLIE: Quincey . . .

QUINCEY: It's true, isn't it?

ELLIE: It was four years ago. The administration has changed. There are some radical groups on campus now.

QUINCEY: The faculty's still in the closet.

MARGO: Ellie tells me there's a professed Communist on the staff. That's a far cry from my college days.

QUINCEY: There may be a two-headed donkey, too, but there sure as hell aren't any homosexuals!

ELLIE: It's a conservative school. This is a conservative state.

QUINCEY: Somebody has to make change happen. Somebody who believes in the goodness of themselves, of what they are.

PAT: So do it.

QUINCEY: (*Frantically*) I can't. I want to be honest and free and proud . . . Everything I do reflects on Ellie.

ELLIE: Quincey, that's enough. (QUINCEY *turns and runs upstairs to the bedroom.*) She's not used to drinking.

MARGO: She seems to be really upset.

ELLIE: I'll go. (*Follows* QUINCEY *upstairs.*)

MARGO: (*To* PAT) Well. I'm not sure I know what all that was about.

PAT: I expect you do.

MARGO: Young people are all crusaders these days.

PAT: Come on, Margo. Don't give me that "Lawsy, Miss Scarlett, I don't know nothing about birthing babies" act.

MARGO: I don't know what you're talking about. (*Rises.*) I'd better check on the spaghetti. I hope Quincey will feel like eating. I made enough for six people. (*She passes the window.*) See? I told you it looked like snow.

PAT: (*Looking out window*) Well, I'll be damned.

   (MARGO *goes to kitchen, leaving* PAT *in living room.* PAT *pours another drink. Upstairs:*)

ELLIE: Quincey . . .

QUINCEY: Why'd you put her in our room?

ELLIE: It's the nicest room. She's a special guest.

QUINCEY: You really want to impress her, don't you?

ELLIE: I did.

QUINCEY: I'm sorry. I couldn't help it. I didn't say anything about you.

ELLIE: If she doesn't know, she's retarded.

QUINCEY: What difference does it make? She may be, herself. If she's not, so what? I love you. I want the world to know it.

ELLIE: I could lose my job.

QUINCEY: Oh, Ellie.

ELLIE: It makes people uncomfortable. They don't understand.

QUINCEY: It's time we made them understand.

ELLIE: Quincey, I know you're right.

QUINCEY: Then, why won't you do something about it? Aren't you proud? Don't you like yourself?

ELLIE: I like being a woman.

QUINCEY: A woman who loves other women.

ELLIE: Quincey, listen to me! When I was your age, "lesbian" was a dictionary word used only to frighten teen-age girls and parents. Mothers fainted, fathers became violent, landlords evicted you, and nobody would hire you. A lesbian was like a vampire: she looked in the mirror and there was no reflection.

QUINCEY: You're scared.

ELLIE: Of course I'm scared. I don't want to be different. I don't want people pointing fingers at me, misguided altruists feeling sorry for me.

QUINCEY: You're a VIP on campus. You could be a figurehead.

ELLIE: I don't have the courage to be a figurehead, Quincey. I'm sorry. (*She starts to leave.*)

QUINCEY: Ellie? I hope I didn't screw things up for you. I don't want to hurt you. I love you. I love you, love you, love you. (ELLIE *holds her.*) It's just that I'm so fucking tired of living in a closet!

ELLIE: (*Pause.*) Are you going to be all right?

QUINCEY: As long as I'm here.

ELLIE: Think you can come downstairs?

QUINCEY: Give me a minute. (ELLIE *releases her, starts to leave.*) I'm sorry.

ELLIE: So am I.

QUINCEY: Someday.

ELLIE: I hope so. (*She comes down the stairs, into the kitchen. To* MARGO) She's all right. Just a little too much to drink. She'll be down for supper.

MARGO: Good.

ELLIE: Can I help?

MARGO: In a minute.

(ELLIE *goes into living room.*)

ELLIE: It's snowing.

PAT: Hard and fast. So I was wrong. I'm not often wrong.

ELLIE: You'd better go right after supper, Pat. I don't want you marooned here all night.

PAT: Don't worry. I've got four-wheel drive. Is the kid all right?

ELLIE: She's not a kid.

PAT: Sorry. Is the young woman all right?

ELLIE: She'll be fine. She doesn't have your tolerance for alcohol.

PAT: She doesn't have my experience.

ELLIE: Thank God.

PAT: You're not in love with her.

ELLIE: I love her.

PAT: It's not the same thing.

ELLIE: It's a lot more reliable.

PAT: What are you going to do, bounce her off your knee when you hear the wind chimes again? Dump her?

ELLIE: No. I'm not going to hurt her.

PAT: You won't be able to help yourself. (*Pause.*) I'd rather you stay with Quincey.

ELLIE: What?

PAT: I'll still have a chance then.

ELLIE: Stop it.

PAT: That one (*Indicating kitchen*) is real competition. I don't want to see that happen.

ELLIE: You don't have anything to do with it.

PAT: Don't I?

(*From the kitchen:*)

MARGO: Okay, set the table!

(ELLIE *begins to do so,* PAT *pours another drink in the living room.* QUINCEY *comes down the stairs,* PAT *sees her, motions her in.*)

PAT: How're you feeling?

QUINCEY: Better.

PAT: This stuff is poison. You got to work up a tolerance, takes years.

QUINCEY: You ought to know.

PAT: What are you going to do?

QUINCEY: About what?

PAT: Your celebrity rival in there.

QUINCEY: She's no rival.

PAT: I wouldn't jump to that conclusion.

QUINCEY: Ellie says you're a troublemaker.

PAT: Do you believe everything Ellie says?

QUINCEY: Most of it. She's as honest as she can be. She wouldn't hurt me.

PAT: She wouldn't mean to. (*Pause.*) I know a game that will nip that in the bud.

QUINCEY: No games. I don't play games.

PAT: It's your funeral.

QUINCEY: (*Pause.*) What is the game?

PAT: I'll come on to you, see. She'll get jealous . . .

QUINCEY: No.

PAT: It'll work.

QUINCEY: No.

PAT: Couldn't hurt.

QUINCEY: No. I won't play games with Ellie.

(ELLIE *enters.*)

PAT: We're getting to know each other.

ELLIE: How about earning your supper?

QUINCEY: I'll get the flatware.

PAT: Want another drink first, Quincey?

ELLIE: She's had enough.

PAT: Oh, listen to Mommy.

QUINCEY: I don't want another drink.

ELLIE: (*At window*) It's really coming down.

(PAT *is at bar.*)

PAT: A late snow. Something like a last chance, wouldn't you say?

(MARGO *enters.*)

MARGO: What was that?

PAT: A late snow. Something like a last chance.

MARGO: (*Pause.*) I suppose so.

(*Car lights outside, a horn.*)

ELLIE: What's that?

QUINCEY: (*At back door*) A car outside.

MARGO: A stranded motorist, probably. The roads must be slippery.

(*A voice calls,* "Ellie!")

ELLIE: (*At door*) Who is it?

VOICE: (*Offstage*) Ellie, I've been driving for hours. I thought I'd never find you. I know I should have called but I just couldn't. I hope you don't mind.

ELLIE: Peggy! (PEGGY*'s at the door.*) Peggy!

(PEGGY *pours into* ELLIE*'s arms.*)

PEGGY: I'm so glad to see you. I thought I was going to slide into a ditch, it's like driving on glass and my snow tires are old, they hardly have any tread. . . .

ELLIE: You look just the same.

PEGGY: You're lying. I look older.

ELLIE: A year or two.

PEGGY: (*Handing* ELLIE *her suitcase*) Here. Is it just terrible of me to come barging in?

ELLIE: No. Of course not.

PEGGY: I didn't have time to call. I walked out on Jim again. The second time this year. I just got in the car, I didn't know where I was going, then I remembered your letter was in my pocketbook, so I followed the directions and here I am. The directions were very good, I usually get lost a dozen times.

ELLIE: Come in.

PEGGY: Oh, you've got company. How stupid of me. I should have called, shouldn't I?

ELLIE: This is Pat, Quincey, Margo, Peggy.

PAT: Perfect Peggy. What do you know.

PEGGY: What?

PAT: Ellie used to talk about you—a lot. I called you Perfect Peggy. (*Pause.*) Forget it.

MARGO: Nice to meet you.

QUINCEY: Hi.

MARGO: Fortunately, we have plenty of food. Join us.

ELLIE: There's a guest bedroom, off to the right, upstairs. Can you manage that?

PEGGY: I managed to get it down the stairs, I guess I can get it up.

ELLIE: Make yourself comfortable, I'll be right up. (PEGGY *goes up the stairs. To* QUINCEY, PAT, MARGO) Can you handle everything down here?

PAT: I don't know. It's getting damned complicated.

MARGO: Go ahead. Five minutes till supper.

ELLIE: I'm sorry about all this, Margo.

MARGO: One has to learn to roll with the punches. I'm rather enjoying it; it's quite educational.

ELLIE: I'll figure something out.

MARGO: I'm sure you will.

(MARGO *smiles as* ELLIE *mounts the stairs.*

PAT *is at the window with* QUINCEY.)

PAT: The trouble with a late snow is—it's unexpected and messy as hell.

CURTAIN

ACT TWO

MARGO *is lying down in the living room, reading. Outside the noise of grinding gears and an occasional "Push!" "Rock it!" from* PAT *and* QUINCEY.

ELLIE *and* PEGGY *are in the kitchen, finishing dishes.*

It is dark outside.

PEGGY: . . . The first three or four years were good, Ellie. I had the kids, we bought the house, we had dreams. Jimmy was the bright young man in college, you remember.

ELLIE: I remember. "Most likely to succeed." Most popular girl weds boy "most likely."

PEGGY: Well, the world is full of colleges and every year thousands of young men, all of them "most likely," descend on the corporate world, swarming towards offices labeled "Executive Vice-President" like salmon dashing for the mating grounds. Head of Northeastern Sales is as far as Jimmy got.

ELLIE: That sounds impressive.

PEGGY: Not to Jimmy. It's a middle-management job. Nobody gets promoted from there. Jimmy says it's the slot reserved for failures. Eight years ago, he quit. He opened his own business. We borrowed from his folks and my folks and we took the kids' tuition money we'd saved—he opened a luxury hardware business.

ELLIE: Luxury hardware?

PEGGY: You know, fancy shelves, early American doorknobs, drawer pulls, drop latches, indirect lighting systems, self-stick bulletin boards, velvet contact paper.

ELLIE: Luxury hardware.

PEGGY: Jimmy has always been farsighted. The time was ripe. So many people living in apartments now, doing their own decorating.

ELLIE: Luxury hardware.

PEGGY: Listen, it was a good idea. Unfortunately, the manager of Woolworth's dime store across the street was also farsighted and sold the same merchandise for 8 percent less. Jimmy went back to Hamilton Die, Head of Northeastern Sales. He thinks of himself as a failure.

ELLIE: And you?

PEGGY: (*Not responding*) I've been working at a thrift shop downtown, four days a week. Lois is a senior this year. She wants to go to Bard but it's out of the question. They only give half scholarships. If she works this summer, between her salary and mine, we'll just be able to get her through a year at State.

ELLIE: You wanted a house on Mulhaven Drive with a maid and a garden out back. In the driveway . . .

PEGGY: (*Joining in the litany*) . . . the *circular* driveway . . .

ELLIE: . . . lined with towering elms . . .

PEGGY: . . . and paved with . . .

ELLIE: Gold.

PEGGY: No. Slate.

ELLIE: You'd sit in the late afternoon, your exquisite straw hat casting perfect shadows on your perfect features. . . .

PEGGY: . . . sipping tall, cool drinks . . .

ELLIE: . . . served on a silver tray, while planning that evening's formal dinner for the town dignitaries . . .

PEGGY: . . . and considering how someone in my position could help the less fortunate.

ELLIE: The fairy princess.

PEGGY: (*Laughing*) No. "Most popular girl weds boy most likely." I never got my circular drive: we have a carport—and a cleaning woman once a week.

ELLIE: Dreams rarely come true.

PEGGY: Yours did. You wanted to teach in a university.

ELLIE: You thought it was a dull, old-maid thing to do.

PEGGY: And to live in a funky apartment with mobiles and wall hangings.

ELLIE: I do.

PEGGY: And to have a funny shack somewhere to get away from it all.

ELLIE: This is it.

PEGGY: Your dreams came true.

ELLIE: Not wholly. I wanted someone to share it with, someone to be a part of it, from the beginning to the end. I always wanted that.

PEGGY: Well, you can't have everything. You got the most important part.

ELLIE: Did I?

PEGGY: And you did it yourself. You didn't depend on someone else. I could never have done that.

ELLIE: Of course you could.

PEGGY: No. I could never have done that. (*She laughs.*) The curse of a fairy princess.

ELLIE: Remember how we used to go over the want ads on Sunday mornings. You were going to be a buyer for the fanciest store in town and I was going to teach. We'd live in a town house with high ceilings and hanging plants—

PEGGY: And mobiles and wall hangings? No, not me. That was you. I never wanted that.

ELLIE: Sometimes you did.

PEGGY: Never.

ELLIE: But the circular drive with the towering elms won out.

PEGGY: Actually, it's a development.

ELLIE: With a carport.

PEGGY: Yes. But it's my life. Mine and Jimmy's.

ELLIE: Why did you leave?

PEGGY: Eddie's at military school. Jim's father pays the tuition. "Make a man out of him." Frankly, I think it's making a jerk out of him. He's so damned disciplined, he doesn't know how to be a kid. Twelve years old and he gives orders like a five-star general. He won't stop at Head of Northeastern Sales.

ELLIE: Why did you leave, Peggy?

PEGGY: When a man thinks he's failed in business, he has to succeed somewhere. His job takes him on the road a lot so he has plenty of opportunity. I've never said a word about it, it's been going on for years. Oh, I haven't been lonely. I have a friend, Wanda. She works with me at the thrift shop. We go out to dinner and to the movies together. I've found letters from his girl friends and phone numbers in his wallet. He hasn't been home for a birthday or anniversary in years but I never accused him. I never accused him. How dare he accuse me!

ELLIE: Of having an affair?

PEGGY: How dare he?

ELLIE: Have you?

PEGGY: Why should he care if I did?

ELLIE: Did you?

PEGGY: He says, if you've thought about it, it's the same as doing it. I haven't done it!

ELLIE: You obviously want to.

PEGGY: Wanda thinks I should leave him.

ELLIE: What do you think?

PEGGY: I think he's a son of a bitch. I've put most of my life into this marriage. The kids will be out of school in a few years. I don't know. I don't know what I want. I guess that's why I came here. You're the only person I know who'll understand. You and Wanda.

ELLIE: (*Meaningfully*) Wanda?

PEGGY: You sound like Jim! Wanda is my friend, like you were my friend. I love her, like I loved you.

ELLIE: We loved each other—a step beyond friendship.

PEGGY: We were friends. Best friends. I never felt so close to anyone, until Wanda.

ELLIE: What you're feeling isn't friendship, Peggy. What we felt together wasn't friendship.

PEGGY: Of course it was! We loved each other.

ELLIE: We were in love with each other.

PEGGY: I'm not like that.

ELLIE: We made love.

PEGGY: That's not true!

ELLIE: Not often, we were both too scared. But we did make love. After the Saint Patrick's Party, New Year's Eve in New Hampshire, your birthday our senior year—I remember every time. I remember it because it was new and pure and perfect. It was always exciting, to the very end it was exciting. It was perfect.

PEGGY: You were going with Danny Rogers and I was going with Morton Tate—until the end of our senior year when I met Jim. We were good friends, Ellie. That's all. (*Pause.*)Danny Rogers is an assemblyman now. They say he's going to run for Congress. You missed a good bet. He married a mouse.

(*The door opens and* QUINCEY *and* PAT *enter, coats drenched from the snow.*)

QUINCEY: No luck.

PAT: We pushed and rocked and spun. It's already four inches and icing up. Nobody's going anywhere tonight.

PEGGY: Too bad Jim's not here. He could get it out.

ELLIE: You may not believe that this drunken women is an ace mechanic, but she is. If Pat can't move that car, nobody can.

PEGGY: I've always felt that men were just naturally better suited for some things.

QUINCEY: I don't believe I heard that.

PAT: (*Flirting with* PEGGY) She doesn't have a wart behind her ear. Has she been picking her nose?

PEGGY: What?

ELLIE: Never mind. Take off that wet coat, Quincey.

PAT: *(To* QUINCEY) Mind Mama. (*To* PEGGY) Want a drink?

PEGGY: Why not?

PAT: Follow me.

(*They go into living room.*)

MARGO: And?

PAT: Can't budge it. Want a drink?

MARGO: No, thanks. I've got coffee.

PAT: Party pooper. Now, what do you want, Perfect Peggy?

PEGGY: An after-dinner drink would be fine.

PAT: Ugh.

PEGGY: Creme de cocoa.

PAT: Really?

PEGGY: I like it.

PAT: I'll see if there's some in the kitchen. (*Goes to kitchen.*)

PEGGY: Excuse me. I hope you won't think I'm rude but . . . (MARGO *looks up.*) are you one of them?

MARGO: I beg your pardon?

PEGGY: You know. One of them.

MARGO: One of what?

PEGGY: Do you like men?

MARGO: Some men.

PEGGY: Do you sleep with them?

MARGO: Men?

PEGGY: Yes.

MARGO: I've probably slept with more men than you've ever met.

PEGGY: Oh, good. It looks like we're all going to have to stay over. You and I can share a room.

PAT: (*Entering with bottle*) That's the first proposition of the night.

PEGGY: (*About bottle, quickly*) That looks fine. That's a very good brand.

PAT: Nothing but the best, baby. Nothing but the best.

(*In the kitchen:*)

QUINCEY: Are you all right?

ELLIE: I'm worried.

QUINCEY: About Pat?

ELLIE: Who's going to be the victim. It's Pat's pattern. Step One: Seduce somebody. Step Two: Hurt somebody else by doing it. It's called "See how much everybody loves me? Anybody who loves me deserves to be punished."

QUINCEY: She wanted me to play a game with her.

ELLIE: A game?

QUINCEY: To pretend I was attracted to her, to Pat. It was supposed to make you pay attention to me.

ELLIE: (*Smiling*) I know that game. It's designed not to make me pay attention to you—but to her.

QUINCEY: I don't understand.

ELLIE: You're too honest. I hope you never understand.

QUINCEY: Something's happening and I'm frightened.

(*In the living room.*)

PEGGY: Are you really an auto mechanic?

PAT: Nope. I'm an antique dealer. A multifaceted human being.

PEGGY: I love antiques. Do you do appraisals?

PAT: Sure. Where do you live?

PEGGY: Oh, I'm too far. About seventy miles.

PAT: I travel.

PEGGY: Maybe you could recommend someone in my area.

PAT: You left your husband, huh?

PEGGY: I need some time to think things over.

PAT: You're bored.

PEGGY: I don't think so.

PAT: You're bored with him, with your marriage.

PEGGY: Maybe I am.

PAT: It happens to everybody. How long have you been bored?

PEGGY: (*Laughs.*) About ten years.

PAT: When the kids started school.

PEGGY: How do you know?

PAT: I've heard it before. I've known a few disgruntled wives.

PEGGY: I'm not just a disgruntled wife. There's a lot more to it.

PAT: There always is.

MARGO: (*Irritated, rises.*) Excuse me. (*She goes upstairs, into the bathroom.*)

PAT: Tell me about you and Ellie.

PEGGY: We were good friends.

PAT: She says you were the most beautiful girl in the school.

PEGGY: My daughter looks just like me. She's beautiful. (*Smiles.*) Things change.

PAT: You're probably more beautiful now.

PEGGY: You are drunk.

PAT: I think women get better with age. Like good wine . . .

PEGGY: Ellie got prettier. She was gawky in college. I never went through that gawky stage. I guess I'm going through it now.

PAT: She really loved you.

PEGGY: We were good friends.

PAT: Romeo and Juliet, Damon and Pythias, Jonathan and David, Gertrude and Alice . . .

PEGGY: We were good friends.

PAT: Nobody could ever live up to you.

PEGGY: No. We were friends. Not that I'm passing judgment on your lifestyle, but we were just friends.

PAT: That's all.

PEGGY: That's all.

PAT: Another creme de cocoa?

(*In the kitchen:*)

QUINCEY: Let's go to bed. Let's just go upstairs and go to bed and let them all do whatever it is that they're going to do.

ELLIE: I can't. When Pat is drunk, she not only plays her games — she's also likely to set the house on fire, turn on the gas without lighting it, leave the grate off the fireplace, fall through the storm door.

QUINCEY: I don't understand why you stayed with her for five years.

ELLIE: It wasn't always like this. Sometimes she'd go for months without drinking. When we were first together, she hardly drank at all. We were so happy and so much in love—and when the drinking started again, I knew what it could be like, what we could have together—and I kept hoping it would come back. I suppose I thought it was my fault.

QUINCEY: It wasn't.

ELLIE: No. It's just the way life is. The wind chimes stop.

QUINCEY: Wind chimes?

ELLIE: The excitement goes, the thrill, the lust, whatever you want to call it.

QUINCEY: But that's just the beginning. That's when a relationship starts: when you stop lusting and start loving.

ELLIE: Is it?

QUINCEY: You have to work at it.

ELLIE: How would you know? You've never had a relationship. You've gone from college affair to college affair.

QUINCEY: We're a relationship.

ELLIE: You've stopped lusting?

QUINCEY: (*Grins.*) Not entirely. When I first saw you at campus orientation, my knees shook. You were at a picnic table, hostessing. I sat down on the grass about twenty yards away and stared. I stared for two hours. For four years, I stared. You were my fantasy. When I finally got into a class of yours, my first grad year, your face was drawn and pained. Your hands shook. I wanted to run to the front of the room and hold you in my arms.

ELLIE: I remember that day. It was the day after the accident.

QUINCEY: I watched you fall apart that year, piece by piece—and piece by piece, put yourself back together: stronger. I loved you for five years before I made love to you. And even then, your thoughts were somewhere else. I know that. I don't care. You're mine now.

ELLIE: Quincey. Go on to bed, honey.

QUINCEY: Where?

ELLIE: In my room. I'll have to move Margo.

QUINCEY: You can't do that.

ELLIE: Would you rather sleep with Perfect Peggy?

QUINCEY: I'd rather sleep with you. In our room.

ELLIE: I'll be up as soon as I get Pat settled.

QUINCEY: Not too long.

ELLIE: At the rate she's drinking, she won't be able to stand up much longer.

(QUINCEY *goes upstairs,* ELLIE *goes into living room.*)

PEGGY: Come on in, Ellie. Have a drink. Pat and I were discussing old times.

PAT: (*To* ELLIE) Your old times. (*To* PEGGY) Ellie doesn't drink.

PEGGY: I remember when she did. On the front porch of the frat house, you drank half a pint of Bourbon and did God-knows-what with Sammy Kincaid and while poor Danny was out beating the bushes for you.

ELLIE: That's why I don't drink.

PAT: Peggy says your college days together were right out of *A Date with Judy*—Jane Powell and Shirley Temple, giggling girl friends.

PEGGY: Well, Ellie did have a crush on me. I remember that. You were very jealous of Jim.

ELLIE: Of course I was!

PAT: And you used to give me the answers in Economics III. I only took that course because all the brightest boys did.

ELLIE: The most-likely-to-succeeds? (*Pause.*) Morty wanted to sleep with you and you told him you couldn't because you were in love with me.

PEGGY: He was a creep. I wanted to shock him.

ELLIE: He spread it all over the campus.

PEGGY: It was a kick. Well, it wasn't true. Anyone who knew me, knew that.

ELLIE: I didn't.

PEGGY: The jocks used to line up in the lounge to see me.

ELLIE: Yes. And Saint Patrick's night our sophomore year, you got into my bed.

PEGGY: I was drunk. I thought you were Jim.

ELLIE: You hadn't even met Jim then.

PEGGY: Well, I thought you were Morty.

PAT: Morty was a creep.

ELLIE: New Year's Eve. Remember New Year's Eve? You were engaged to Jim. At midnight, everybody kissed. You didn't kiss Jim. You kissed me. In front of the whole fucking fraternity house. Jim walked out. You didn't see him again until spring semester.

PEGGY: I didn't meet him until spring semester.

PAT: Will the real Perfect Peggy please stand up?

PEGGY: It didn't happen! Not like that.

ELLIE: It did. And it's happening again. With Wanda.

PEGGY: I'm not a lesbian! (*She runs upstairs to the guest bedroom, stage left.*)

PAT: It wasn't real.

ELLIE: It was!

PAT: Even if it happened, it wasn't real. Unadmitted, without commitment.

ELLIE: It was so perfect.

PAT: You never faced the bills together, you never faced joblessness together, you never built a house together, a life together. You never faced death together. It wasn't real. We were real.

ELLIE: We didn't work.

PAT: Why? I don't know why. I love you.

ELLIE: You don't love you.

PAT: All right. I never wanted to be a woman. It's a crappy thing to be. You can't do anything! I saw my father raking in the money, playing big business, flying to Europe, to the Caribbean, buying booze and women in every part of the globe while my mother ran the diaper brigade for eight kids. She never got farther than the corner A&P. Her conversation was limited to baby talk and what she heard on the radio. My father met Al Capone—met him! While my mother was scrubbing underwear on a washboard. Here's your choice, kiddies. Which one would you rather be?

ELLIE: Your father was a crook. What's good about that?

PAT: Is a crook. A successful one. The main man in Boston. My mother's dead of a heart attack.

ELLIE: I didn't know.

PAT: Last year.

ELLIE: I didn't know.

PAT: It doesn't matter. She's been dead for forty years. We finally buried her. But he goes on. And so do I. And I don't know why anymore. . . . Give us a chance, Ellie.

ELLIE: It's too late.

PAT: Can't you remember how it was? We built a home together: we made love on that beach at midnight and sailed that broken-down boat under the stars until dawn. We were safe from the world.

ELLIE: For a while.

PAT: Then you started teaching. You were gone so much, seeing new people. That's why I went out with other women, Ellie. To make you know how much you loved me.

ELLIE: The wind chimes stopped. And we didn't know how to make it work. Too much has happened. We can't go back.

PAT: Let me come home, Ellie.

ELLIE: I'm sorry. This isn't your home anymore.

(PAT *lunges for the front door and exits as* MARGO *comes down the stairs.*)

MARGO: (*To* PAT) Hey! It's cold out there. (*To* ELLIE) Shouldn't you go after her?

ELLIE: She's safer outside than in. She's very drunk, Margo. She'll wander around in the snow until she gets cold and wet enough to come in. As long as she can't move the car, she's safe.

MARGO: You know her very well.

ELLIE: I thought I did.

MARGO: Are you still in love with her? (ELLIE *turns, shocked.*) I'm not blind.

ELLIE: I'm sorry. I didn't intend to bring you into all of this.

MARGO: Are you?

ELLIE: I love her. I remember being in love with her. (*Pause.*) No.

MARGO: Quincey?

ELLIE: She loves me.

MARGO: That wasn't the question.

ELLIE: Quincey says that once the thrill goes, when the knees stop trembling and the wind chimes stop tinkling, it's a job. You've got to work at it.

MARGO: She's right.

ELLIE: Pat and I didn't know how to do that.

MARGO: But Quincey does.

ELLIE: Probably. But I think you have to hear chimes first.

MARGO: And you haven't?

ELLIE: Not with Quincey. I love her. I appreciate her, I'm thankful for her. But no chimes. Ever.

MARGO: I was married to a man once, much like Pat. Worse, I guess. He was not only a drunk but a violent drunk. And I loved him. I loved him long after I left him. And I loved again. A woman. She died ten years ago.

ELLIE: (*Surprised*) I'm sorry.

MARGO: I haven't written a publishable book since that time. I haven't let another human being touch me since that time. Oh, I've slept with a few. I picked up a salesman in the bar downstairs from my hotel room. He was from Detroit. I never saw him again. Another time, a bellhop. And a woman reporter from a newspaper upstate. She was in town for the afternoon to interview me. But they didn't touch me: not emotionally, not really physically. I made love to them. . . . It's hard to make anything last, Ellie. A job, a talent, a marriage.

ELLIE: A lot of people do it.

MARGO: A lot of people hold on to dead things. But to make something last—and live . . . It's harder with a woman. There are no rules. And the stakes are so very high. (*They look at each other for a moment.*) We worked at it. We worked very hard at it. We brought new things into our relationship, we challenged one another with ideas, with goals. We weren't always successful. We had bad years, years when I was sure it was over, when I thought it should be over. But we survived them, somehow. It was good again, it was working. (*Pause.*) I think I hated her for dying, for leaving me. And I was very frightened. I still am.

ELLIE: But you've learned to be alone.

MARGO: I don't do it very well. I need to share, to be a part of something.

ELLIE: But they don't last. It doesn't last. You start to build—and it's over. You start again—and it's over. Why bother?

MARGO: Because you need it. I need it. And we keep hoping, all of us: men and women, women and women, men and men, that we can make it work. What do you want, Ellie?

ELLIE: Someone to grow with. Someone to build with.

MARGO: You can do that with Quincey. What do you want, Ellie?

ELLIE: I want it all. I want to tremble. I want that kind of crazy desire that surmounts reason. I want someone to live for, to die with. Someone to climb mountains for, slay dragons for, someone to snuggle with by a fire when the world is cold. I want a lover consumed by the greatest passion, a partner possessed of the greatest loyalty, a friend committed to the greatest love.

With Pat, there was passion. With Quincey, there is loyalty. I don't want to settle. I want it all.

I thought I'd had it all with Peggy. Passion, loyalty, friendship. I thought it had been perfect. But it was so long ago and I was so young. I knew less than. Maybe I needed less, too.

MARGO: Does she remember it as perfect?

ELLIE: She doesn't remember it at all.

(QUINCEY *appears at the head of the stairs.*)

QUINCEY: Are you coming up?

ELLIE: In a minute.

(QUINCEY *comes down the stairs.*)

QUINCEY: Where's Pat?

MARGO: She's outside. Waiting for spring.

QUINCEY: Is she all right?

ELLIE: I want to wait and see. Go back to bed, honey. I'll be up in a minute.

QUINCEY: Okay. Hurry. (*She goes back up the stairs.*)

MARGO: What are you going to do, Ellie?

ELLIE: I don't want to hurt anybody.

MARGO: Why did you ask me here?

ELLIE: (*Pause.*) Because I liked you.

MARGO: Liked me?

ELLIE: Because I felt something. The night we talked in my hotel room, I felt something.

MARGO: What?

ELLIE: I don't know. Something. A beginning.

MARGO: And what are you going to do about it?

ELLIE: (*Pause.*) Wait.

MARGO: Why?

ELLIE: Because I'm scared. Because I'm tonguetied when I talk to you, and my knees feel weak. When I stand near you there's electricity between us like a living thing. Because something great is growing here and I'm afraid for it to start. I don't want it to end. And I don't know what you want.

MARGO: (*After a long moment*) I want you. (*Holds out her arms.*) Don't settle, Ellie.

(ELLIE *goes into* MARGO's *arms as* PAT *comes quietly in the back door, wet and drunken. She sees what is happening and sneaks quietly up the stairs to* PEGGY's *room.* PEGGY *is staring out the window at the lake.*)

PAT: Hi, there.

PEGGY: It's the abominable snowman.

PAT: The boat has a hole in it.

(*From the bedroom:*)

QUINCEY: Ellie?

(*In the living room:*)

ELLIE: (*To* MARGO) I've got to go.

MARGO: Not yet.

(*Upstairs:*)

PAT: (*Crossing the hallway to* QUINCEY's *room*) Hi.

QUINCEY: Hi.

PAT: (*Explaining*) The boat has a hole in it.

QUINCEY: What?

PAT: Ellie wants you downstairs.

(QUINCEY *gets up as* PAT *goes back to* PEGGY's *room.*)

PEGGY: Don't sit on the bed. You're all wet.

PAT: You want me to take them off?

PEGGY: No!

(*Downstairs:*)

MARGO: You've got to make a decision, Ellie.

(*Upstairs:*)

PAT: I will if you will.

PEGGY: Stop it! (*She starts to cry.*)

PAT: Hey, I'm sorry.

(*Downstairs:*)

MARGO: I have something at stake here, too, you know. I have everything at stake.

(*Upstairs:*)

PAT: Come on, cut the waterworks.

PEGGY: Hold me. Please hold me. I'm so afraid.

PAT: (*Doing it*) Perfect Peggy.

(QUINCEY *comes down the stairs, unsuspectingly turns the corner.*)

QUINCEY: Ellie? (*She sees* ELLIE *and* MARGO. *Turns, runs up the stairs.*)

ELLIE: Quincey!

QUINCEY: No! (*She runs into the room, slams and locks the door.* ELLIE *follows.*)

ELLIE: Quincey! Quincey?

QUINCEY: No!

MARGO: (*At the foot of the stairs*) Leave her alone, Ellie.

(ELLIE *slowly comes down the steps. As the lights in the upstairs room dim to black. ELLIE and MARGO move to the sofa in the firelight. They lie down together and the firelight slowly dims then cross fades to dawn.*)

PAT: Rise and shine! (QUINCEY *in her room and* PEGGY *in hers hear and rise and hurriedly begin to dress.*) The birds are chirping, the sun is shining and the late snow is melting into spring.

MARGO: (*Sitting up*) Why aren't you hung over?

ELLIE: (*Sleepily*) She never is.

MARGO: It's criminal.

PAT: Rise and shine, Ellie, put on the coffee! We itinerants have to get packing.

MARGO: Make it yourself, you chauvinist pig.

ELLIE: Believe me, you wouldn't want to drink it.

(PAT*'s in the kitchen, getting the pot out.*)

PAT: The pot, coffee, measuring cup: all ready! (ELLIE *rises, goes to the kitchen.* PAT *countercrosses to the living room. To* MARGO) Sleep well?

MARGO: Fine, thank you. What about you? Did you sleep in the snow?

PAT: I came in. (*Pause.*) Upstairs with Perfect Peggy.

MARGO: You're very sure of yourself, aren't you?

PAT: Not at all. I know what I want.

MARGO: Not Peggy.

PAT: Not Peggy. . . . I'm a gambler. Are you?

MARGO: No.

PAT: I can tell. Your odds are bad. She's a three-time loser. And I know the track. Are you betting win, place, or show?

MARGO: Across the board.

PAT: Want some advice?

MARGO: No.

PAT: Come back to town with me. I'll take you to dinner, we'll get to know each other. I'm a very interesting person.

MARGO: (*Smiles.*) No.

PAT: I'd make a great character for a book. You can study me.

MARGO: (*Smiles.*) No.

PAT: I can't take you out of the running, huh?

MARGO: (*Smiles.*) No.

(ELLIE *has put on the coffee and goes upstairs. She knocks on* QUINCEY's *door.*)

ELLIE: Quincey?

PAT: I'm going out to start the car. But I'm not going far. Ever.

(*Upstairs:*)

ELLIE: Quincey.

(QUINCEY *unlocks the door, admits* ELLIE.

Downstairs:)

PAT: Consider yourself warned.

(*Upstairs:*)

ELLIE: Quincey.

QUINCEY: That's why you brought her here.

ELLIE: No.

QUINCEY: It wasn't enough in Philadelphia.

ELLIE: That's not how it happened.

QUINCEY: And Chicago and Des Moines and how many other cities, how many other conferences, how many other business trips? I've been sitting home like an idiot, believing you.

ELLIE: It never happened before.

QUINCEY: What was I? A convenient place to rest?

ELLIE: I wanted it to work with us, Quincey.

QUINCEY: You never worked at it. My whole life is constructed around you. I can't write what I want to, it reflects on you. I can't be who I am, you'll lose your job. "May I ask someone home for supper?

May I have the key to the cabin? May I use the car? May I, may I, may I?" Ellie decides everything. What Ellie wants, what Ellie needs, how Ellie wants to live. I don't even exist!

ELLIE: I'm sorry.

QUINCEY: Sorry isn't good enough! You made a commitment to me!

ELLIE: I didn't want to. Do you remember that? I didn't want to.

QUINCEY: I thought you'd learn to love me.

ELLIE: I wanted to. I really wanted to.

QUINCEY: We're good together!

ELLIE: No. It isn't enough, Quincey. It's bad for me—it's bad for you. You have so much love to give.

QUINCEY: I love you.

ELLIE: I love you. But not the right way.

QUINCEY: Is this just an affair? A week? A month? I'll wait.

ELLIE: No.

QUINCEY: I'm good for you.

ELLIE: But I'm not good for you. You're young, you can be free, you can be open, you can build the kind of life you want. You can fight for what you believe in. You can make a difference, Quincey. There's a world of women out there, young women, who'll stand with you.

QUINCEY: I want you.

ELLIE: I can't.

QUINCEY: Are you in love with her?

ELLIE: I don't know yet. I think so.

QUINCEY: Then you're not in love with me. You've never been in love with me. (*Pause.*) I guess I've always known that. I thought I could make it happen.

ELLIE: I never lied to you.

QUINCEY: Not in words. By holding me, living with me, making love to me. You lied to me. (*She hits the wind chimes at the window.*) I heard them. You didn't. You used me. That's the most degrading part of all.

ELLIE: I'm sorry.

QUINCEY: I have some sweaters and things in the drawers. I'd like to pack them. (*Pause.*) Can I use that duffel bag?

ELLIE: (*Nods. Going to her.*) Quincey . . .

QUINCEY: (*Pulling away*) For God's sake, leave me with some dignity.

(ELLIE *backs from the room, watching* QUINCEY *for a moment, then closes the door.*

PEGGY *comes out of the bathroom, dressed.*)

PEGGY: Good morning. (*She goes into her bedroom, gets her suitcase.*) Ready to go. Hope I can get my car out.

ELLIE: You're leaving?

PEGGY: I'm going home.

ELLIE: Oh.

PEGGY: I have a life there. It's not what I had in mind, but it's mine.

ELLIE: With Jim?

PEGGY: He won't change. Neither can I.

ELLIE: And Wanda?

PEGGY: Wanda is my friend. That's all. That's the way it's going to stay. I can't deal with it, Ellie. It takes courage: a kind I haven't got.

ELLIE: You came here for help. I'm afraid I didn't offer much.

PEGGY: I came looking for an answer. An answer that worked for me. I found it. I have a nice house, two lovely children, a good job. I'll settle for that. (*She proceeds down the stairs with her suitcase.*)

(PAT *enters from the yard.*)

PAT: Car's started. We'll have no problem getting out.

PEGGY: What about mine?

PAT: It's only a couple of feet from the road.

PEGGY: Would you do it for me?

PAT: My pleasure.

PEGGY: Now.

PAT: Don't you want a cup of coffee first?

PEGGY: I'll stop on the road. I want to go home. Before I change my mind. (*She extends her hand.*) Ellie, thanks. Don't go to any more New Year's Eve parties. It gets everybody in a lot of trouble.

(PEGGY *and* PAT *exit.*

QUINCEY *comes down the stairs, carrying the duffel bag. She and* ELLIE *look at one another for a minute.*)

QUINCEY: I want the apartment. I decorated it and I want it.

ELLIE: (*Meekly*) All right.

QUINCEY: Call me when you want to pick up your things. I won't be there. (*She pauses, looks at the Dutch cupboard, touches it.*) To remember me by. (*She looks at* MARGO.) I suppose I'll see you around campus. (*She crosses to the door.*) Work at it. (*She exits.*)

ELLIE: Will we have this moment?

MARGO: There are no guarantees.

ELLIE: Perfect Peggy settled.

MARGO: Some people have to. (*Pause.*) And some people can't.

(ELLIE *pours a cup of coffee and hands it to* MARGO.)

ELLIE: The snow's almost gone.

(PAT *enters brightly, takes the coffee out of* MARGO's *hand, sips it.*)

PAT: Thanks. Well, Peggy's on her way. You always had good taste, Ellie. (*She pockets a piece of paper.*) Her phone number. She needs an occasional appraisal. (*She gulps the rest of* MARGO's *coffee, hands her the empty cup.*) Quincey's waiting in the car.

ELLIE: Thanks for delivering the hutch.

PAT: It's okay. I overcharged her. (*To* MARGO) Across the board?

MARGO: Across the board.

PAT: I'll be waiting at the finish line. (*She kisses* ELLIE *on the cheek.*) See you soon, Ellie.

ELLIE: No.

PAT: (*Shaking* MARGO's *hand*) Good luck.

MARGO: We're running on a long track, Pat.

PAT: I've got a lot of patience.

> (PAT *exits.*
>
> ELLIE *watches them go.*
>
> MARGO *pours two cups of coffee.*)

MARGO: Black?

ELLIE: Fine.

MARGO: (*Gives the coffee to* ELLIE.) Where will you live?

ELLIE: I'll find an apartment.

MARGO: I'll need to live near campus. How would that look, our living together?

ELLIE: Do you care?

MARGO: No.

ELLIE: Neither do I. I'm tired of living a half-life.

MARGO: So am I.

ELLIE: I can't march. But I won't hide. (*She moves to window.*) What's your favorite color?

MARGO: Blue.

ELLIE: Favorite flower?

MARGO: Marigold.

ELLIE: Favorite season?

MARGO: Summer.

ELLIE: Favorite food?

MARGO: Pineapple.

ELLIE: Pineapple?

MARGO: (*Smiling*) Pomegranate?

(*Both are at the window.*)

ELLIE: The snow is gone. The sun is out. (*She opens the window.*) Favorite person? (*The wind chimes tinkle in the breeze. They both laugh. MARGO holds out her arms.*) Let's try to keep it that way. (*The lights fade in the foreground until the two women are silhouetted in the morning sun.*)

CURTAIN

OTHER BOOKS FROM
T 'n' T CLASSICS, INC.

from **Jane Chambers:**
MY BLUE HEAVEN - her happiest, lightest, most antic excursion into hysteria - when a gay couple is mistakenly named couple of the year. An utter delight! PLAY with 1 man and 2 women   only $7.95

BURNING - hauntings and harrowing experiences, love and laughter merge in an absorbing novel from a most sensitive writer. Her first NOVEL, recently re-issued $9.95

CHASIN' JASON - a romp ready for the millenium, that will leave you breathless. Let your imagination loose and your laughter flow free!   NOVEL $9.95

WARRIOR AT REST poems that trace the writer's life and loves.   POETRY $6.95

OTHER AUTHORS
DORIC WILSON
STREET THEATRE - **The Stonewall Riots presented as they are recalled by an activist who was there. 10 males, 2 females, 2 female impersonators. PLAY $7.95**

PERFECT RELATIONSHIP leathermen and disco mavens in conflict, resulting in roomies becoming more than friends. 4 men, 1 woman   PLAY $7.95

FOREVER AFTER a vivisection of gay male love -without intermission 4 male actors   PLAY $7.95

SIDNEY MORRIS' *IF THIS ISN'T LOVE* - a lifelong love between two fascinating men   PLAY $ 7.95

and a few remaining copies of: the plays:
Arch Brown's *NEWS BOY* $5.95
C.D. Arnold's **THE DINOSAUR PLAYS** $6.95
Robert Chesley's *STRAY DOG STORY* $7.95

JANE CHAMBERS'
LAST SUMMER AT BLUEFISH COVE
from the early reviews:

"Chambers can write!"   New York Magazine

"Confronted with a play as lovely and funny and sad as Jane Chambers' LAST SUMMER AT BLUFISH COVE, a critic finds that words fail. Chambers is...supplying the need... for a lesbian/feminist voice in the theatre.

OTHER STAGES

"Drama at its best"   SOHO NEWS

"The play is a joy for lesbians and a revelation for hetero-sexual women. What a relief to see lesbians portrayed as serious and silly, strong and weak, superficial and sensitive, grasping and generous."   WOMANEWS

"One of the finest scripts in recent seasons."
Washington Blade

"A tight, truthful script, by turns wonderfully funny and painfully sad, that holds its own with the best writing around town today."   N. Y. DAILY NEWS

"Excellent play...rewarding experience"
WOR-TV

"A warmhearted play about love and death...the play is so appealing that everybody will probably still be on the beach come winter."   NEW YORK POST

"An important and loving work."
MICHAEL'S THING

T 'n' T Classics Inc.
P.O. BOX 1243 ANSONIA STATION
NEW YORK N Y 10029
212-736-6279; 212-595-3004
FAX 212-695-3219

YOUR NAME_____

COMPANY_____

ADDRESS_____

CITY_____STATE_____ ZIP_____

QTY	TITLE	AUTHOR	LST EA	DSCT	PRICE

SUBTOTAL_____

TAX_____

SHIPPING_____

TOTAL_____

ORDERING INSTRUCTIONS:

NO CASH THROUGH MAIL, PLEASE. We accept checks and American Express, outside u.s., american express only. make checks payable to:

T 'n' T Classics Inc. P O Box 1243 Ansonia Station

New York, N Y 10023

DELIVERY: ALLOW 2 WEEKS EXCEPT ON EXPRESS ORDERS. POSTAGE & HANDLING $3.00 - ONE OR TWO SOFT COVER BOOKS; $4.00 FOR 3 BOOKS; ADD $1.00 SJIPPING AND HANDLING EACH ADDITIONAL BOOK. sENT MAIL OR UPS. WE CAN EXPRESS DELIVER IN NEW YORK CITY WITHIN 48 HOURS FOR $12 FEE. EXPRESS ELSEWHERE: YOU PAY ADDITIONAL COSTS. SHIPPING CHARGES OUTSIDE COUNTRY DETERMINED BY WEIGHT. INDIVIDUAL ORDERS: NEW YORK RESIDENTS, PLEASE ADD 8.25 % TAX.

CREDIT CARD_____

EXPIRATION DATE_____YOUR SIGNATURE_____